PRAISE FOR

JESUS UNVEILED

"As I read the first chapter, I began to realize that this is an important book—not only for me personally—but for the entire church and for the growing house church movement. I believe that this book has the potential to be used to train church planters all over the world."

— KEN EASTBURN, FORMER NATIONAL DIRECTOR OF
HOUSE2HOUSE MINISTRIES

"[*Jesus Unveiled*] gives a clear call for us to 'go out of business' and be the Family outlined in the New Testament. Perhaps the most beautiful part of this book is the invitation to live in the mystery of The Body of Christ. Giles fully challenges us without sending us running. He sheds light on such a beautiful Bride that I am drawn in more deeply and vow again to live in a mystery of family, love, submission, provision, grace, and healing. This book gives me courage to hope that the Body of Christ really can transform our world."

— CRISSY BROOKS, FORMER EXECUTIVE DIRECTOR AND
CO-FOUNDER OF MIKA CDC

"It has been such an encouragement to my heart in the past fifteen years to see one book after another critique the status quo, challenge assumed traditions, and present a fresh vision for a functioning Body of Christ on earth. The Bride of Christ is such a beautiful and multifaceted organism that the nuances and insights that each author brings to the table can never exhaust the riches Christ has deposited in his Ekklesia on earth. This is another wonderful, refreshing addition to the collection of writings in our generation that will help believers practice Christ-centered assembly life."

– JON ZENS, AUTHOR OF *A CHURCH BUILDING EVERY ½ MILE*
AND EDITOR OF *SEARCHING TOGETHER* MAGAZINE

"Skimmed it. Looks good."

– FRANK VIOLA, AUTHOR OF *PAGAN CHRISTIANITY*

"In this book, Keith Giles presents us with the powerful example of his own life as he has dared to live out the prophetic insights he has discovered into the nature and mission of God's culture-challenging community. Read and gain courage to risk following his inspired and dynamic servant-leadership."

– DR SCOTT BARTCHY, PROFESSOR OF CHRISTIAN ORIGINS AND
THE HISTORY OF RELIGION IN THE DEPARTMENT OF HISTORY,
UCLA

"This is a refreshing book on the growing house church movement. It offers some personal and practical insights, provides a fresh look at the scriptures about the form and function of the church, and would be a good introductory read to those asking questions about whether God is calling them into this spiritual revolution."

— RAD ZDERO, AUTHOR OF *LETTERS TO THE HOUSE CHURCH MOVEMENT*

"This is a much-needed treatise about the state of the church in North America. My hope is that this book will become required reading in seminaries and Bible colleges across the land. Unfortunately, it's more likely that it will be added to the bonfire by the hoity-toity elite who see their security being threatened."

— KENT WILLIAMSON, DIRECTOR OF *REBELLION OF THOUGHT*, FOUNDER OF PALADIN PICTURES, INC.

"Giles calls the church back from its preoccupation with business models and encourages believers to embrace spiritual relationships with one another and dependence on the Holy Spirit as we read about in Scripture."

— ALAN KNOX, BLOGGER AND DOCTORAL STUDENT, BIBLICAL THEOLOGY

OTHER BOOKS BY THE AUTHOR

Available online at: www.KeithGiles.com

Copyright © 2019 by Keith Giles.

First published as *This Is My Body: Ekklesia As God Intended*, 2010 by Subversive Press, Orange, California.

Additional material includes: "Anatomy of an Organic Church," "Pitfalls of Organic Church," and "What's Wrong With House Church," published online at www.subversive1.blogspot.com by Keith Giles.

This edition is expanded, updated, and edited to reflect the transforming views of the author on this important subject.

Cover design and layout by Rafael Polendo (polendo.net)

ISBN 978-1-938480-42-3

This volume is printed on acid free paper and meets ANSI Z39.48 standards.

Printed in the United States of America

 QUOIR

Published by Quoir
Orange, California

www.quoir.com

JESUS
UNVEILED

FORSAKING CHURCH AS WE KNOW IT FOR EKKLESIA AS GOD INTENDED

KEITH GILES

DEDICATION

This book is dedicated to my wife,
and my very best friend, Wendy. You're my
inspiration on this grand adventure.

SPECIAL THANKS

Without the tireless and constant assistance
of Jon Zens, this book might never have seen
print. Thanks for your encouragement
and your hard work.

TABLE OF CONTENTS

FOREWORD

Have you ever walked out of a Sunday morning church service feeling like something was missing? I'm not saying the music wasn't good or the sermon wasn't interesting. I'm just asking: did you ever drive home afterward, wondering if the experience could have been something so much more?

Does it ever seem, in all our big productions and all our busyness *about* Jesus—our songs about Jesus, our sermons about Jesus, our choir practices, church plays, and children's programs about Jesus—the one thing that's missing is a profound, life-changing experience *with* Jesus?

I'm not saying each of us hasn't had some kind of experience with Jesus in the past. But is that all our church gatherings are about? Wouldn't we rather have an opportunity to experience him again, right now, rather than continuously reminiscing about a previous encounter we once had?

If so, then I'm really glad you picked up this book. This isn't a book about how to have a meeting *about* Jesus; it's a book about how to have meeting *with* Jesus. And it isn't just based on theory; it's based on actual experience. Hard-earned, life-lived, real-world experience.

My buddy Keith Giles has walked the talk. Among other things, he started a ministry which hosted weekly church services for economically disadvantaged families, living in an old motel. Other churches soon joined, and it eventually spawned a nationwide "motel church" ministry.

An ordained minister, Keith walked away from his livelihood and church-as-usual to start a house church which gave away 100% of all funds collected. This church also served the homeless Tent City community in Orange, California and sent people out who felt called to plant more house churches in the U.S. and overseas, and to serve the poor and marginalized in various places and cultures.

Furthermore, Keith served on the board of *House 2 House Ministries* (an international house church non-profit ministry founded by John and Felicity Dale), and helped re-launch their *House 2 House Magazine* online. Plus, he's written several articles and blog posts, recorded videos and podcasts, and spoken at numerous events on the subject of house church/organic church.

However, this isn't just another book on house church. If anything, it's more like three books in one. The book begins with Keith making a very passionate, exciting, and thoroughly biblical case for returning to a simpler, more authentic way of experiencing Christ in church community.

But the book doesn't stop there. Not wanting to leave the reader with unrealistic and overly-romanticized ideas about house church, Keith brings his years of experience to bear on the shortcomings and mistakes many of us have made in pursuing this form of church community.

And not to spoil anything, but this part of the book is a very transparent and much-needed confession. My hope is that Keith's honesty and insight here will heal a lot of hurts on both sides of the divide between all us house church folks and our brothers and sisters in the institutional church.

Honestly, if Keith had stopped there, this book would already be very valuable and I would have no problem recommending you read it. But the book becomes truly indispensable as it moves into its final sections because it's here that Keith gets into the nitty-gritty "how to" stuff.

Some house church proponents (myself, included) often tend to shy away from the "how to" stuff. And that's very understandable. No one wants their well-intentioned advice to become distorted into some kind of formula for the "right way" to do church.

But avoiding such questions is simply erring on the other side. Unless believers see how truly simple this whole endeavor can be, they will never become confident enough to step out of the box. And this is where I get most excited for you. Because I know the practical wisdom Keith provides in the latter sections of this book is going to empower so many of you.

Not to overstate things, but this is actually a very big moment for some of you. Up to this point, the Lord has been leading you to this particular crossroads. And yes, it's okay if you read this book and go back to life-as-normal in an institutional church somewhere. At the very least, reading this book will have given you a better understanding of your brothers and sisters who have chosen a very different path when it comes to their church experience.

However—and I'm not afraid to put my own personal bias on display here—for those of you who choose "the road less traveled", an amazing adventure awaits. Many of you are going to experience Jesus in ways you never thought possible. Your relationships with him and with other believers are going to become so much deeper, your friendships so much more intimate. Not to mention, you're going to have a much greater impact on those around you.

If you've ever walked out of a Sunday morning church service feeling like something was missing, if you ever wondered if your church experience could have been something so much more, this book is about to confirm all those suspicions. But more importantly, it's going to serve as your roadmap for finding the kind of church experience you've been longing for.

– Richard Jacobson

Author of *Unchurching: Christianity Without Churchianity*

"PROPERLY SPEAKING, NEW TESTAMENT CHRISTIANITY KNOWS NOTHING OF THE WORD 'SACRAMENT,' WHICH BELONGS ESSENTIALLY TO THE HEATHEN WORLD OF THE GRAECO-ROMAN EMPIRE AND WHICH UNFORTUNATELY SOME OF THE REFORMERS UNTHINKINGLY TOOK OVER FROM EKKLESIASTICAL TRADITION. FOR THIS WORD, AND STILL MORE THE OVERTONES WHICH IT CONVEYS, IS THE STARTING POINT FOR THOSE DISASTROUS DEVELOPMENTS WHICH BEGAN SOON TO TRANSFORM THE COMMUNITY OF JESUS INTO THE CHURCH WHICH IS FIRST AND FOREMOST A SACRAMENTAL CHURCH."

—EMIL BRUNNER

INTRODUCTION

I know that many who read this will find it hard to believe, but my inspiration for writing this book is founded in my love for the Church. Because of this love I cannot sit by silently and watch her wallow in her own complacency and ignorance. I cannot allow her to settle for less than all that her loving Creator has intended for her to experience. I cannot allow her to feast on the food she has scavenged from the spiritual dumpster when I can plainly see the table spread before her, filled with homemade delicacies freshly prepared and placed there for her sustenance.

The Church in the West is desperately in need of a revival. She has languished for so long in the seat of comfort and complacency that there is a desperate need for her to be awakened, and refreshed, and renewed from within. She has forsaken her calling. She has forgotten her name. She has been seduced by the shiny things of this fallen world and, worst of all, she has been distracted to the point of forgetting her One true love.

In some ways this is a prophetic book. Not in the sense that those who read it may learn the future, but rather in the sense that, by reading it, one might remember the past and return to the original path laid out centuries before by God Himself. At least, this is my dearest hope and prayer.

In the Old Testament, God raised up prophets to remind the Nation of Israel who they were, and by what means they had been saved from slavery and gathered as a people. In the New Testament, Jesus came and fulfilled the Messianic prophecy. He proclaimed the coming of the Kingdom of God and lived a life that demonstrated what citizens of the Kingdom should be like. Today, I feel that we are desperate once again for a prophetic word to shake us from our stupor and awaken us from our slumber. Until those prophets appear, I hope that this book may help us remember some of what we've forgotten about who we are called to be.

One of my favorite quotes is from A.W. Tozer who said, "We must not think of the Church as an anonymous body, a mystical religious abstraction. We Christians are the Church and whatever we do is what the Church is doing. The matter, therefore, is a personal one. Any step forward in the Church must begin with the individual."[1]

This means that, at the most fundamental level, you and I are the Church. There is no way for us to talk about the Church without essentially speaking about ourselves, the followers of Jesus. Because of this, I understand that any criticisms directed at the Church may be painful to hear, however we must allow ourselves to consider the truth, even if it hurts.

I pray that all of those who read this book may extend to me an extra measure of grace as we navigate these sensitive family issues. Please understand that I am very much in love with Jesus. I am also very much concerned about the well-being of the Church we are all a part of. I do not hate the Church. I do not harbor any grudges against any pastor. I do not have any anger in my heart towards the Body and Bride of Christ. Indeed, it is truly out of my passionate love for the Bride that I take the time and energy to hold this mirror to her beautiful face—the face that Jesus loved enough to die for—and to help her cover the bruises, heal the wounds and make herself ready for the Groom who is even now at the door.

If after reading this book you have any questions or desire further interaction with me on a specific topic or subject, I am happy to correspond with you and to engage with you in this important dialog concerning the Bride of Christ and God's design for His Church.

Thank you for taking the time to read this book. I hope and pray that God may use these ideas and thoughts to prepare us all to be the Church that God always dreamed of.

Sincerely,
– **Keith Giles**

CHAPTER 1

GOD'S DESIGN FOR HIS EKKLESIA

EKKLESIA AS GOD INTENDED

Whenever we engage in dialog about the New Testament form of church it is inevitable that someone will suggest that there is no New Testament model for what the church is supposed to look like. I want to affirm to you that nothing could be further from the truth.

My very purpose for writing this book is to make clear that God most certainly does have a specific design for His New Testament Church. Furthermore, I believe that it is essential for us, as followers of Christ, to do our best to understand this design. Why? Because the design is not arbitrary or accidental in nature. God's design for His Church is embedded in the very fabric and spiritual DNA of the Gospel itself.

At face value, I think we should acknowledge that the very idea that God has no strong opinion about how His Church should operate or function is contrary to His character.

Did God remain aloof when it came to the design of the Tabernacle? Was He indifferent to how the Temple was to be constructed? On the contrary, God was meticulous and specific concerning his design for both the Tabernacle and the Temple under the Old Covenant. Why, then, should we assume that He suddenly has no intention or design for His New Testament Church?

GOD WAS METICULOUS AND SPECIFIC CONCERNING HIS DESIGN FOR BOTH THE TABERNACLE AND THE TEMPLE UNDER THE OLD COVENANT. WHY, THEN, SHOULD WE ASSUME THAT HE SUDDENLY HAS NO INTENTION OR DESIGN FOR HIS NEW TESTAMENT CHURCH?

Furthermore, we must agree that it would be more than a little odd for God to take the time to inspire the entire New Testament—which chronicles the birth and formation of the Church—and not also reveal to us anything about what that Church should look like, or how it should function, or what form it should take.

What I am speaking of here are not merely my opinions. These are clearly revealed facts documented in both the Old and New Testaments, under the inspiration of the Holy Spirit, concerning God's ultimate plan for His people—the Body of Christ.

My hope is that everyone who claims to follow Christ would take seriously these very specific and clearly communicated designs that God Himself has revealed to us by His Spirit and in His Word.

More than this, my prayer is that we would not only see what God has to say about His design for His Church, but that we would also be willing to explore all that He has for us to experience in this new pattern.

GOD'S NEW TEMPLE

To understand God's design for His New Testament Church, we have to look at the Old Testament. Specifically, we must look for prophecies given by God about a new temple, and we must try to understand what He was trying to accomplish in raising it up.

One of the most startling prophecies concerning the Messiah and his role in establishing this new temple is found in Zechariah.

> "Listen, O high priest Joshua and your associates seated before you, who are men symbolic of things to come: I am going to bring my servant, the Branch." (Zechariah 3:8)

In this passage, God speaks to the high priest of Israel at this time whose name was translated "Joshua." Of course, we know that this name is synonymous with "Y'shua" or "Jesus" and this is not an accident. God points out the significance of this to Zechariah, saying:

> "The word of the LORD came to me: 'Take the silver and gold....and make a crown, and set it on the head of the high priest, Joshua son of Jehozadak. Tell him this is what the LORD 20 Almighty says: 'Here is the man whose name is the Branch, and he will branch out from his place and build the temple of the LORD.'" (Zechariah 6:9-12)

Several significant things can be said about this remarkable passage. First, God asks Zechariah to fashion a crown of silver and gold and place it on the head of "Y'shua" the high priest. By doing this, God is declaring that this priest is to also be crowned as a king.

Secondly, God confirms that the Branch, or the Messiah, will have the name "Y'shua" or "Jesus." Notice, it is his name which is the Branch.

Remember, God has already revealed that "Y'shua" the high priest is a man "symbolic of things to come" and part of this symbolism is revealed in his name.

Therefore, these prophecies in Zechariah teach us that the Messiah who is to come will be a priest and a king, and his name will be Jesus, and also that:

"It is he who will build the temple of the Lord, and he will be clothed with majesty and will sit and rule on his throne. And he will be a priest on his throne. And there will be harmony between the two.' (Zechariah 6:13)

CLEARLY, THIS SCRIPTURE TELLS US THAT BUILDING THE TEMPLE OF THE LORD WAS PART OF THE MISSION OF THE COMING MESSIAH, AND THAT HIS IDENTITY AS A PRIEST AND A KING WOULD HAVE SIGNIFICANCE IN HIS KINGDOM.

Clearly, this scripture tells us that building the temple of the Lord was part of the mission of the coming Messiah, and that his identity as a priest and a king would have significance in his kingdom.

In 2 Samuel we read where King David looked around his opulent cedar palace and concluded that it wasn't right that he should live in such splendor while God lived in a tent outside the city.

"After the king was settled in his palace and the Lord had given him rest from all his enemies around him, he said to Nathan the prophet, 'Here I am, living in a palace of cedar, while the ark of God remains in a tent.' Nathan replied to the king, 'Whatever you have in mind, go ahead and do it, for the Lord is with you.'" (2 Samuel 7:1)

When David tells the prophet Nathan that he intends to build a house for God the prophet enthusiastically tells David that he is certain God will be with him no matter what he plans to do.

However, that very night God nudges Nathan and gives him a surprising response to David's request.

"Go and tell my servant David, 'This is what the LORD says: Are you the one to build me a house to dwell in? I have not dwelt in a house from the day I brought the Israelites up out of Egypt to this day. I have been moving from place to place with a tent as my dwelling. Wherever I have moved with all the Israelites, did I ever say to any of their rulers whom I commanded to shepherd my people Israel, 'Why have you not built me a house of cedar?'" (2 Samuel 1:5-7)

Here, God questions whether David, or anyone else, is capable of building a house for God to dwell in. As God says later through the prophet Isaiah, "Heaven is my throne, and the earth is my footstool. Where is the house you will build for me? Where will my resting place be?" (Isaiah 66:1) Instead, God tells David something startling:

> "The LORD declares to you that the LORD himself will establish a house for you. When your days are over and you rest with your fathers, I will raise up your offspring to succeed you, who will come from your own body, and I will establish his kingdom. He is the one who will build a house for my Name, and I will establish the throne of his kingdom forever. I will be his father, and he will be my son." (2 Samuel 7:11-14)

Not only will God not allow David to build Him a house, God is promising that He, the Lord Himself, would build a house for David. His promise is that, through the Messiah who would come from the Davidic bloodline, God would build a house for His Name and establish a kingdom that would last forever.

Clearly, from this passage and from the Zechariah passage we see confirmation of a Messianic calling to build the temple of God. More than this, God is clear that only the Messiah is qualified to build the temple he requires. This temple, as revealed in both passages above, is tied to the identity of the Messiah as a priest and a king who sits upon a throne which lasts forever and who rules over a kingdom that never ends.

THIS TEMPLE, AS REVEALED IN BOTH PASSAGES ABOVE, IS TIED TO THE IDENTITY OF THE MESSIAH AS A PRIEST AND A KING WHO SITS UPON A THRONE WHICH LASTS FOREVER AND WHO RULES OVER A KINGDOM THAT NEVER ENDS.

The Old Testament scriptures not only point to a Messianic temple being built, but to the passing away of the Levitical model of worship. One of the more startling examples of this is found in the book of Jeremiah.

> "In those days, when your numbers have increased greatly in the land," declares the LORD, "men will no longer say, 'The ark of the covenant of the LORD.' It will never enter their minds or be remembered; it will not be missed, nor will another one be made. At that time they will call Jerusalem 'The Throne of the LORD', and all nations will gather in Jerusalem to honor the name of the LORD. No longer will they follow the stubbornness of their evil hearts." (Jeremiah 3:16-17)

In this passage, God speaks of a time that is coming when no one will speak the name of the ark of the covenant, nor will it be remembered or missed or rebuilt. Why would this happen? How could this possibly be?

The ark of the covenant was the place where the Holy Presence of God rested. It rested behind the thick veil of the tabernacle, and, eventually, within the temple itself in Jerusalem. Only the high priest could enter in at specific times to offer the sacrifice for God's people. No one else was permitted to stand before the ark of the covenant, and even the priest who stood near it was in danger of falling dead if he failed to deal with his own sin accordingly.

The ark of the covenant was central to Jewish temple worship. It represented the presence of the Living God as dwelling among His people. Without it, the entire meaning of the temple, the priesthood and the sacrifice was in question.

Yet, God tells us that the day is coming when the ark, and all it represents will be forgotten, and never remembered or spoken of again among God's people. Even though the ark is absent, the nations of the earth gather to honor the name of the Lord and to worship God. In fact, the city of Jerusalem itself is identified as the throne of the Lord, or "the place where God dwells and reigns."

One can easily imagine how confusing, and even troubling this passage might be to a Jewish believer who has placed so much faith in the established system of temple worship. Yet, God is clearly communicating His intention to replace the old testament temple system of worship with something radically different. In other words, it will not look like what has been seen or understood to this point. The elements and the patterns of worship in this new temple of God will not mimic what has gone before.

In his book, "The Temple and the Church's Mission", Dr. G.K. Beale writes, concerning the Jeremiah passage above:

> "The reason the ark in the temple is not remembered is that a greater temple than the more physical one will encompass not only all of Jerusalem but the entire world. This future temple will be so incomparably greater than the former that God's people will not even 'remember it nor shall they miss it'. Furthermore, a physical ark within a small temple will 'not be made again' because everything to which it pointed has been realized."

Another passage which can help us to understand the prophecy in Jeremiah is found in the book of Joel where God says:

> "I will pour out my Spirit on all people. Your sons and daughters will prophesy, your old men will dream dreams, your young men will see visions. Even on my servants, both men and women, I will pour out my Spirit in those days." (Joel 2:28-29)

Obviously, if God's Spirit is poured out on all people, the need for a physical ark where God's presence dwells is eliminated. Moses himself dreamt of such a day when he said:

> "I wish that all the LORD's people were prophets and that the LORD would put his Spirit on them!" (Numbers 11:29)

In Daniel 2:44-45, King Nebuchadnezzar's dream about the future is interpreted for us:

> "In the time of those kings, the God of heaven will set up a kingdom that will never be destroyed, nor will it be left to another people. It will crush all those kingdoms and bring them to an end, but it will itself endure forever. This is the meaning of the vision of the rock cut out of a mountain, but not by human hands—a rock that broke the iron, the bronze, the clay, the silver and the gold to pieces."

This prophecy reveals that God's kingdom will be established, first as a small stone, cut from the rock, "but not by human hands", and that it will grow to destroy every earthly kingdom and it will "never be destroyed" but "it will itself endure forever."

From each of these passages we can see a pattern emerging. God is promising to send a Messiah. He will be a priest and a king. He will sit upon a throne which will last forever. This same king will come from the lineage of King David and he will be the one to build a temple for God. This new temple will not require an ark of the covenant to symbolize God's presence among His people. Instead, the Spirit of God will be poured out upon all flesh and it will be so glorious that no one who experiences this will ever long to return to the old way of worship. The old covenant will be fulfilled, and a new covenant will replace it.

OLD TESTAMENT TEMPLE WORSHIP

Now that we've seen God's promise concerning His plan to send a Messiah who would build a new temple, let's take a moment to explore key elements of Jewish Temple worship. By understanding the basic elements of the Old Testament form of worship, we can better understand how the New Testament fulfillment of these prophecies stand in contrast to what has gone before.

The basic elements of the Old Testament form of worship include the temple, the priesthood, and the daily sacrifice.

Each of these elements is crucial to the Old Testament model for worship. By examining these we can get a better context for how the promised Messiah would fulfill each of them, and establish a new, and more complete, paradigm for worship.

First, let's look at the temple of God. The temple of God is the Holy Place. It's where the Spirit of the Living God dwells. Usually, in the Old Testament, God's presence is connected to the ark of the covenant, as we have already seen. The temple is where those who are hungry to meet with God go to connect with Him.

"I was glad when they said to me, 'Let us go into the house of the Lord.'" (Psalm 122:1)

The temple in its most simplistic form is simply the place where the presence of God dwells. Throughout the Old Testament we are given several types of temple forms. The first is the Garden of Eden. From the very beginning God reveals to us His original intention—to make his dwelling place with mankind. The Garden of Eden is a type of temple because God is seen walking with Adam and Eve in the cool of the day. He visits with them and speaks to them in an intimate manner.

Another type of temple in the Old Testament is the mountain. Abraham's testing of his faith takes place upon Mount Moriah. Noah offers sacrifices to God on Mount Ararat. God first speaks to Moses on Mount Horeb, "…the mountain of God" (Exodus 3:1) and later, God also speaks to Moses at Mount Sinai and gives the people the ten commandments. At this time, the early forms of the tabernacle, and later the temple itself, are revealed. God appears in the form of a cloud at the top of the mountain. Only Moses is allowed to ascend the mountain and meet with

God. The people are told not to touch the mountain itself or they will die, much like the later command not to touch the ark of the covenant. (See Exodus 19).

The tabernacle, which literally means, "dwelling place" was another early form of temple. It was constructed according to God's specific instructions (See Exodus 36) and was built to house the ark of the covenant. The tabernacle was an impermanent, easily portable construction which moved with the Jewish people as they wandered in the desert before entering the promised land.

Finally the temple built by Solomon (1 Kings 6) is also a type of temple which points us to the ultimate, final temple which the Messiah will build for God.

The second element of Old Testament temple worship is the sacrifice. This blood sacrifice of an animal upon the altar in the temple was for the covering of sins against God and against others. (See Numbers, chapter 15).

Typically, a lamb without blemish would be brought into the temple and offered upon the altar as an atonement offering to God for sins. Once offered, the sacrifice provided a return to fellowship with God and access to the temple, and God's presence.

The final element in the Old Testament model of worship is the priesthood. According to the scriptures, the priests were set apart to God. Only a priest was allowed to serve in God's temple and perform the necessary sacrifices. They are also the only ones who, through a process of purification, were deemed worthy to enter the "Holy of Holies"—where the ark of the covenant rested behind a thick veil—and approach God's presence.

Priests are the ones who hear God's voice and communicate God's message to those who are outside the Temple. The priests are primarily concerned with the spiritual health and education of God's people. To be a priest was both a great honor, and a serious responsibility.

The Old Testament model of worship utilized these three key elements; the temple, the sacrifice, and the priesthood. However, as we have already seen, God's promise concerning the Messiah was that He would build a new temple, one where the ark of the covenant was not central. As radical as this seems, the implication is that God's presence would no longer remain in a single geographical location, yet His Spirit would fill the new temple. Therefore, the new temple which was to be built by the Messiah would not be located in a single geographic location.

> THE OLD TESTAMENT MODEL OF WORSHIP UTILIZED THESE THREE KEY ELEMENTS; THE TEMPLE, THE SACRIFICE, AND THE PRIESTHOOD. HOWEVER, AS WE HAVE ALREADY SEEN, GOD'S PROMISE CONCERNING THE MESSIAH WAS THAT HE WOULD BUILD A NEW TEMPLE, ONE WHERE THE ARK OF THE COVENANT WAS NOT CENTRAL.

The implication would seem to be that for the Messiah to accomplish his calling, he would have to bring an end to the practices of the Old Covenant, and we know that the only way to bring these practices to an end would be to fulfill them.

> "But the ministry Jesus has received is as superior to theirs as the covenant of which he is mediator is superior to the old one, and it is founded on better promises. For if there had been nothing wrong with that first covenant, no place would have been sought for another." (Hebrews 8:6-7)

Under the New Covenant, these forms are fulfilled, or fully realized, and they cease to become necessary. They are shadows which point to what has already come.

Once these shadows are fulfilled they no longer serve any further purpose. Instead, the focus must shift to the promise fulfilled, and to the one who has fulfilled the promise.

THE LIGHT REMOVES THE SHADOW

Have you ever wondered at the apparent difference between the way God behaved in the Old Testament and the way Jesus reveals Him in the Gospels? Perhaps you yourself have struggled with this apparent contradiction of character. Is there a logical explanation for why God seems to be so bloodthirsty and vengeful in the Old Testament scriptures, and yet so loving and gentle in the New Testament?

Well, this debate is as old as Christianity itself. In fact, the very first person to point out this difference was Jesus himself.

In the Gospel of Matthew, chapter 5, Jesus quotes the Old Covenant and then makes a new proclamation that demonstrates the differences between the two.

First, he points out the differences in the Old Covenant command "Thou Shalt Not Kill" found in the Law of Moses and provides a radical new command under the New Covenant:

"You have heard that it was said to the people long ago, 'Do not murder, and anyone who murders will be subject to judgment.' But I tell you that anyone who is angry with his brother will be subject to judgment" (Matt 5:22-23)

Here at the start of his sermon on the mount, Jesus lays out for everyone a new covenant perspective which permeates the Good News of the Kingdom he has come to proclaim.

In the past, God operated under the Old Covenant rule which was expressed through the Law of Moses, or the Ten Commandments. Now, according to Jesus, things will be different. As we enter the Kingdom of God, we can now expect something new. Instead of "Do not murder", Jesus ups the ante with "Don't be angry."

Throughout this section of scripture, Jesus continues to contrast specific commands of the Old Covenant with new standards found in the New Covenant of Grace. Having addressed the command about murder, next he addresses "Thou Shalt Not Commit Adultery":

> "You have heard that it was said, 'Do not commit adultery.' But I tell you that anyone who looks at a woman lustfully has already committed adultery with her in his heart." (Matt 5:27-28)

> "It has been said, 'Anyone who divorces his wife must give her a certificate of divorce.' But I tell you that anyone who divorces his wife, except for marital unfaithfulness, causes her to become an adulteress, and anyone who marries the divorced woman commits adultery." (Matt 5:31-32)

Next he addresses the commands against bearing false witness or swearing oaths:

> "Again, you have heard that it was said to the people long ago, 'Do not break your oath, but keep the oaths you have made to the Lord.' But I tell you, Do not swear at all..." (Matt 5:33-34)

Finally, he addresses the Law in the Old Covenant concerning murder and retribution:

> "Jesus said, "You've heard it said, 'An eye for an eye and a tooth for a tooth', but I say to you, do not resist and evil man, and whoever shall strike you on the right cheek, turn to him the other also." (Matt 5:38-39)

> "You have heard that it was said, 'Love your neighbor and hate your enemy.' But I tell you: Love your enemies and pray for those who persecute you, that you may be sons of your Father in heaven." (Matt 5:43-44)

Why do you think Jesus starts off his sermon on the mount by making such a radical set of statements? In effect, he is quoting the Law of the Old Covenant and saying that those things are no longer valid. Instead, he's replacing the commands of the Old Covenant with brand new, Kingdom-centric ideas which go beyond mere obedience. These words of Jesus speak of the heart, not simply about rules to follow.

> "Do not think that I have come to abolish the Law or the Prophets; I have not come to abolish them but to fulfill them." (Matt 5:17)

So, Jesus came to announce the Kingdom of God and to proclaim a New Covenant. He did this, first of all, by fulfilling the Old Covenant. These were but shadows, according to the author of Hebrews:

> "The law is only a shadow of the good things that are coming— not the realities themselves." (Hebrews 10:1)

The New Covenant is not like the Old. So, we shouldn't be surprised at the differences. The Old Covenant has now been fulfilled in Christ, and now that Old Covenant is no longer in effect. It has been fulfilled. Now, we are living under the New Covenant which Jesus came to inaugurate. He is the High Priest of this New Covenant and He has outlined for us, in the Gospel, what life in the Kingdom should look like.

HE IS THE HIGH PRIEST OF THIS NEW COVENANT AND HE HAS OUTLINED FOR US, IN THE GOSPEL, WHAT LIFE IN THE KINGDOM SHOULD LOOK LIKE.

No longer will we live by the code, "An eye for an eye" but now we will live by the new code, "Love your enemies."

The Old Testament and New Testament are not concurrent realities. The Old Covenant is fulfilled in Christ and now we are under a New Covenant. Behold the old is gone and the new has come.

This does not imply that the Old Covenant scriptures are irrelevant at all. These are still valuable to us so that we can comprehend how they were fulfilled in Jesus. But these are still shadows which point to Jesus.

"You diligently study the Scriptures because you think that by them you possess eternal life. These are the Scriptures that testify about me, yet you refuse to come to me to have life." (John 5:39-40)

According to the Old Covenant, God promised to send His Messiah to fulfill the prophecies concerning a New Covenant. This Messiah would be a priest and a king, and he would be the one who would build a temple for God—one not made with human hands.

Throughout the ministry of Jesus, we see him emphasizing the temporal nature of the shadow and the eternal qualities of the Kingdom of God. Specifically, Jesus quite often speaks about the Temple in terms that make the Jewish religious class very nervous.

"Destroy this temple, and in three days I will raise it up." (John 2:19)

Jesus was the fulfillment of the shadow found in the Old Covenant priesthood. He is now our only High Priest.

Jesus was the fulfillment of the shadow of the sacrificial lamb who takes away our sins. We no longer require a blood sacrifice as part of our worship to God.

Jesus was the fulfillment of the shadow of the temple. We no longer need to travel to a physical, geographical holy place to come into the presence of Almighty God.

"One greater than the temple has come," Jesus said in Matthew 12:6. At his crucifixion, God tore the veil in the temple in two, from top to bottom, to signify the end of that old covenant temple system. The priests, the animal sacrifice, and even the temple itself are all now superfluous and unnecessary.

The author of Hebrews summarizes all of this for us when he says:

"When Christ came as *high priest* of the good things that are already here, he went through the greater and *more perfect tabernacle* that is *not man-made*, that is to say, not a part of this creation. He did not enter by means of the blood of goats and calves; but he entered the Most Holy Place once for all *by his own blood*, having obtained eternal redemption." (Hebrews 9:11-12; emphasis mine)

Here we see that Jesus fulfilled the shadows of high priest, temple, and sacrificial lamb. He took the role of High Priest when He offered Himself as the unblemished Lamb of God, in the temple of His body. Thus, Jesus reveals that He was what each of these shadows were pointing to all along. These shadows are all fulfilled in Christ.

But why did Jesus do all of this? What are the practical implications of these actions for those of us who are now living under a New Covenant?

Here's the beautiful symmetry of what Christ accomplished for us: Jesus is our High Priest so that we can become a Kingdom of Priests.

"You have made them to be a kingdom and priests to serve our God, and they will reign on the earth." (Revelation 5:10)

Jesus is the Living Temple of God so that we can become the Temple of the Holy Spirit.

"Do you not know that your body is a temple of the Holy Spirit, who is in you, whom you have received from God? You are not your own." (1 Corinthians 6:19)

Jesus is the Lamb of God so that we can also become living sacrifices to God.

"Therefore, I urge you, brothers, in view of God's mercy, to offer your bodies as living sacrifices, holy and pleasing to God—this is your spiritual act of worship." (Romans 12:1)

In fact, all of this is confirmed in the writings of Peter who says:

> "*As you come to him*, the living Stone—rejected by men but chosen by God and precious to him— *you also, like living stones, are being built into a spiritual house* to be *a holy priesthood, offering spiritual sacrifices* acceptable to God through Jesus Christ…But you are a chosen people, a *royal priesthood*, a holy nation, a people belonging to God, that you may declare the praises of him who called you out of darkness into his wonderful light. Once you were not a people, but now you are the people of God; once you had not received mercy, but now you have received mercy." (1 Peter 2:4-5; 9-10; emphasis added)

As we've already seen, the Messiah was sent, in part, to build a temple for God that was "not made by human hands." Yet, when Jesus walked the Earth, there was already a physical temple standing in Jerusalem. What was the temple that Jesus came to establish? It was you and I—the living temple of the Holy Spirit.

Jesus fulfilled His mission and built a house for God. Jesus alone was the one who fashioned a resting place for His Father. He did what David, and Solomon and all the rest could never do. He built an acceptable temple for God that was cleansed with His own blood and purified by the Lamb of God.

> "For we are the temple of the living God. As God has said: 'I will live with them and walk among them, and I will be their God, and they will be my people.'" (2 Corinthians 6:16)

What is the purpose of a temple? It's a Holy Place. It's where people can go to find God, to approach Him and to enter into His presence.

If you and I are now the temple of God on this earth, this means that whenever people come to you, whether they know it or not, they are standing in front of the temple of the Living God.

"But Christ is faithful as a son over God's house. And we are his house, if we hold on to our courage and the hope of which we boast." (Hebrews 3:6).

THE CHURCH IS MADE ONLY OF LIVING, BREATHING PEOPLE WHO CARRY AROUND WITH THEM THE HOLY PRESENCE OF THE LIVING GOD IN THEIR HEARTS.

Even though we often think of the Church as a building, it is not a building. The Church is an organism, not an organization. The Church is made only of living, breathing people who carry around with them the Holy Presence of the Living God in their hearts.

If you have surrendered your life to Christ, then God lives in you by His Spirit. He has made His home in you, by your faith in Christ Jesus and the finished work of Christ on the cross. This is not a small thing. In fact, the ripping of the veil in Solomon's Temple, the cloth separating God and mankind, was ripped from top to bottom the very instant that Jesus accomplished His work on the cross.

"And when Jesus had cried out again in a loud voice, he gave up his spirit. *At that moment* the curtain of the temple was torn in two from top to bottom." (Matt. 27:50-51).

God did not wait even one second longer than necessary to remove the veil which separated us from Himself. How could we ever again seek to repair this veil and establish again a series of religious barriers between ourselves and God?

We are the only House that God has ever built. We are the only temple ever commissioned by God to house His Holy Presence.

The True and Living God has built for Himself a living, breathing temple on this earth and we are that temple.

So, we see from the Scriptures that it was always God's plan to fulfill the shadows of priesthood, temple and sacrifice through the promised Messiah. When the Messiah came, He revealed that

He was the reality to which these shadows pointed. When Jesus fulfilled these shadows at the cross, they ceased to be necessary. This means we no longer require a special clergy or priestly class of men to operate as a type of Christ for us because the Christ Himself has already come. We no longer require the blood of sheep to cover our sins, because the Lamb of God has already come and offered Himself as the perfect atonement for our sins. We no longer require a special, holy place where we must go to meet with God because God has fulfilled His promise to us and He has made us to be the temple of His Holy Spirit.

I believe that it is for these reasons that the New Testament Church did not seek to build temples where they could worship, or to ordain priests who would act as spiritual mediators, or to offer blood sacrifices on the altar for the forgiveness of sins. They understood that Christ had fulfilled all of these shadows. They fully recognized that they were now the temple of the Holy Spirit. They understood that they themselves were now God's Holy Priesthood, offering themselves to God as daily, living, sacrifices.

> I BELIEVE THAT IT IS FOR THESE REASONS THAT THE NEW TESTAMENT CHURCH DID NOT SEEK TO BUILD TEMPLES WHERE THEY COULD WORSHIP, OR TO ORDAIN PRIESTS WHO WOULD ACT AS SPIRITUAL MEDIATORS, OR TO OFFER BLOOD SACRIFICES ON THE ALTAR FOR THE FORGIVENESS OF SINS. THEY UNDERSTOOD THAT CHRIST HAD FULFILLED ALL OF THESE SHADOWS.

This was not an arbitrary decision. It was not one based upon cultural restrictions, nor did it mirror the Jewish or Pagan systems of the day. Instead, it was an organic model founded upon Christ Himself and revealed in the Holy Scriptures.

Is it any wonder that Jesus cried from the cross, "It is finished!" after accomplishing all of this? The cross of Jesus accomplished so much more for us than forgiveness of sins and eternal life. He fulfilled the promises of the Old Covenant to usher in the ongoing reality of a New Covenant where God's greatest desire could be fully realized.

THE NEW COVENANT OF GOD

From the beginning, God's plan was to make His home with mankind. The first book of the Bible lays out for us God's original design for all of creation and at the center of this is His intimate desire to be with us.

The Garden of Eden was a type of temple—a sanctuary where God and man could fellowship and commune together. After the Fall, the tabernacle and the temple served as shadows which pointed to the one, true temple which was to come—one not made with human hands. The Apostles and the first Christians were thrilled to realize that they were living in the reality of these promises, and they proclaimed it loudly. As Stephen said before he was stoned to death:

> "However, the Most High does not live in houses made by men. As the prophet says: 'Heaven is my throne, and the earth is my footstool. What kind of house will you build for me? says the Lord. Or where will my resting place be? Has not my hand made all these things?'" (Acts 7:48-50)

Paul also echoed this truth when he spoke to the worshippers of the "Unknown God" in Athens saying:

> "The God who made the world and everything in it is the Lord of heaven and earth and does not live in temples built by hands." (Acts 17:24)

The early Christians knew that Jesus had died to fulfill the Old Covenant and rose from the dead to preside over a New Covenant that was promised long ago. The Jewish leaders of the day also fully understood that the preaching of the Gospel posed a threat to their status quo. This is partly why they opposed Stephen and accused him of "speaking against this holy place and against the law." (Acts 6:14) It's also why they opposed Paul and arrested him at the temple in Jerusalem saying, "This is the man who teaches all men everywhere against our people and our law and this place." (Acts 21:28)

In the New Testament we see that many understood that what Jesus had inaugurated was the foundation of a brand new temple "not made with human hands" that made the existing temple obsolete and superfluous.

> "This is the covenant I will make with the house of Israel after that time, declares the Lord. I will put my laws in their minds and write them on their hearts. I will be their God, and they will be my people. No longer will a man teach his neighbor, or a man his brother, saying, 'Know the Lord,' because they will all know me, from the least of them to the greatest. For I will forgive their wickedness and will remember their sins no more." (Jeremiah 31:31-34)

At the feast of Pentecost, the birthday of the New Testament ekklesia, Peter confirmed that what God promised to do in the Old Testament scriptures through the prophet of Joel was being fulfilled in their very presence.

> "'In the last days, God says, I will pour out my Spirit on all people. Your sons and daughters will prophesy, your young men will see visions, your old men will dream dreams. Even on my servants, both men and women, I will pour out my Spirit in those days, and they will prophesy." (Acts 2:17-18)

God's promise was fulfilled at Pentecost. He poured out His Spirit on all flesh—not just on the prophet, not just on the men, but on women, and children, on the old and on the young. This was the inauguration of something radically different than what had gone before.

Later, through both Peter and Paul, God would confirm by His Spirit that this outpouring was not only for the Jews, but also for the Gentiles as well.

> "For there is no difference between Jew and Gentile—the same Lord is Lord of all and richly blesses all who call on him." (Romans 10:12)

> **GOD'S NEW COVENANT WITH MAN WAS NO LONGER CONFINED ONLY TO ONE RACE OF PEOPLE, BUT NOW IT WAS WIDE OPEN TO EVERY LIVING, BREATHING HUMAN BEING ON THE PLANET WHO RESPONDED TO THE OPEN INVITATION OF JESUS TO FOLLOW AFTER HIM.**

"Therefore, remember that formerly you who are Gentiles by birth.... that at that time you were separate from Christ, excluded from citizenship in Israel and foreigners to the covenants of the promise, without hope and without God in the world. But now in Christ Jesus you who once were far away have been brought near through the blood of Christ....His purpose was to create in himself one new man out of the two, thus making peace, and in this one body to reconcile both of them to God through the cross, by which he put to death their hostility. He came and preached peace to you who were far away and peace to those who were near. For through him we both have access to the Father by one Spirit." (Ephesians 2:11-18)

God's New Covenant with man was no longer confined only to one race of people, but now it was wide open to every living, breathing human being on the planet who responded to the open invitation of Jesus to follow after Him.

> "Consequently, you are no longer foreigners and aliens, but fellow citizens with God's people and members of God's household, built on the foundation of the apostles and prophets, with Christ Jesus himself as the chief cornerstone. In him the whole

building is joined together and rises to become a holy temple in the Lord. And in him you too are being built together to become a dwelling in which God lives by his Spirit." (Ephesians 2:19-22)

The new, living, breathing temple of God was now unleashed upon the earth and set free to expand and cover the whole of creation, without limit or boundary. As Jesus promised, "...I will build my church and the gates of hell shall not prevail against it." (Matthew 16:18)

God's New Testament Temple was built upon the Chief Cornerstone, and there is no longer any other "Holy Place" than the heart of every believer, and the collective ekklesia (gathering) of God's people. As Dr. G.K. Beale said to me:

> "Hebrews chapter 9 uses the word parable to refer to the physical Temple (v 8-9). The physical, Old Testament Temple is not the literal Temple. It's the illustrative Temple. The Temple that Jesus has begun to establish is called the "True Temple." So, to look at the picture is not to see the substance that is already here....Christ is the true Israel. He is the true Temple. So, to look longingly at the picture of a physical temple is to make the same mistake. The substance is here, (in Christ)."[1]

As we've already seen, the symbols of the Old Covenant were shadows, not the realities themselves. The shadow of the physical temple was revealed in the true temple of Christ's body. The shadow of the priesthood was revealed in the person of Jesus our High Priest. The shadow of the blood sacrifice was fulfilled in the sacrifice of the Lamb of God who gave Himself for the sins of the world.

What would be the point of going back to the Old Covenant shadows now that the light has come and these things have found fulfillment in Christ?

The Old Covenant model depended on incomplete symbols, whereas the New Covenant model is the true reality. Instead

INSTEAD OF A SELECT GROUP OF MEN SET ASIDE AS MEDIATORS BETWEEN GOD AND MAN, THE NEW COVENANT PRIESTHOOD INCLUDES EVERY MAN, WOMAN AND CHILD IN THE KINGDOM OF GOD. of a select group of men set aside as mediators between God and man, the New Covenant priesthood includes every man, woman and child in the Kingdom of God. Instead of a single, man-made temple in one geographic location, the New Covenant temple has expanded to fill every baptized believer in Christ Jesus. Instead of a blood sacrifice to provide a temporary covering for our sins, we have all been covered in the Blood of the Lamb and we ourselves are now the living sacrifices of God.

We must remember also that the Old Covenant forms of worship were man-made and not God's original desire for His people. When He created all things, God made a place where He would be free to relate to His creation. In the Garden we see God's true heart revealed. Yet this goal was circumvented when mankind made a choice to disobey.

When God brought His people out of Egypt and lead them into the desert and towards the promised land it was the people, not God, who suggested that Moses speak to them on behalf of God.

> "When the people saw the thunder and lightning and heard the trumpet and saw the mountain in smoke, they trembled with fear. They stayed at a distance and said to Moses, 'Speak to us yourself and we will listen. But do not have God speak to us or we will die." (Exodus 20:18-19)

Later, in the days of the prophet Samuel we read how God's people rejected God as their King.

> "But when they said, 'Give us a King to lead us,' this displeased Samuel so he prayed to the Lord. And the Lord told him: Listen to all that the people are saying to you; it is not you they have

rejected, but they have rejected me as their king." (1 Samuel 8:6-7)

It was never God's plan to create divisions between Himself and His people. Instead, it was Adam's sin in the Garden that created the first divide. Then it was the fear of the Israelites in the desert that put a mediator between us and God, and finally it was the desire of a nation to be like "all the other nations" that brought the final rejection of God as King.

The Old Covenant is filled with examples like this where God desires to pull His people closer and His people continually pull back because of fear, and sin, and pride.

But the Good News of the New Covenant is that God has made a way for us to live free of sin. He's made a way for love to cast out all fear. He's promised to give grace to those who are humble.

The New Covenant is the fulfillment of God's glorious dream where "I will be their God and they will be my people."

Does anyone dare to pick up a needle and thread in an attempt to repair the old veil? Would anyone be so foolish as to long for anything less than the complete expression of this new reality we have found in Christ?

Certainly there was a time in history when it was appropriate to build a holy place where a holy man could perform a holy work. But this time has long passed. This shadow has long since been eclipsed by the Light of the World.

To this very day there is no physical Jewish temple of worship in Jerusalem or anywhere else. Why? Because these shadows have served their purpose.

We have a New Covenant now. One where every believer can now be ordained into the priesthood of God, (1 Peter 2:5) and every believer is now the daily, living sacrifice (Romans 12), and every believer is now the temple of the Holy Spirit. (1 Cor 6:19)

EVERY BELIEVER A PRIEST OF GOD

"It was never in the mind of God that a privileged priesthood of sinful, imperfect men would attempt, following the death and triumphant resurrection of our Lord Jesus Christ, to repair the veil and continue their office of mediation between God and man. The letter to the Hebrews makes that fact very plain. When Jesus rose from the dead, the Levitical priesthood, which had served Israel under the Old Covenant, became redundant."

—A.W. TOZER[2]

According to the New Testament, it was never God's plan to have His New Covenant Church operate like a Levitical priesthood. Jesus commanded His disciples not to emulate the top-down organizational structures of either the Jewish religion (Matt 23:8-12), or of the Pagan authorities (Mark 10:42-45). Instead, He urged them to treat one another as brothers and as equals.

Paul, in 1 Corinthians, chapter 12, outlines God's plan for the Church to operate as a Body. In this New Testament model, Jesus is the only Head and the people within the Church are empowered—each and every one of them—by the Holy Spirit to minister to one another.

"Now to each one the manifestation of the Spirit is given for the common good." (1 Corinthians 12:7)

Notice how each of these various gifts are distributed to the Body, by the Holy Spirit for a single purpose: "for the common good." God does this so that everyone in the Body is necessary and so that everyone contributes and shares the burden of ministry.

> "All these are the work of one and the same Spirit, and he gives them to each one, just as he determines." (1 Corinthians 12:11)

Notice that Paul doesn't say, "…he gives them to ONE PERSON" but that these gifts are given to "each one" of the members within the Body.

> "The body is a unit, though it is made up of many parts; and though all its parts are many, they form one body. So it is with Christ." (1 Corinthians 12:12)

Notice how the body is a reflection of Christ himself if we operate as a unit made up of many parts all working together under the headship of Christ. The implication is that if we do not function as God designed, we are not reflecting Christ to the world.

> "For we were all baptized by one Spirit into one body—whether Jews or Greeks, slave or free— and we were all given the one Spirit to drink." (1 Corinthians 12:13)

Notice how throughout 1 Corinthians 12 the emphasis is not on one particular member but on the entire Body itself. This is especially significant when you consider that this church in Corinth was probably one of the most troubled and morally challenged churches in early Christian history. Even so, Paul never abandons the shared body ministry in order to correct these errors. He never commands their elders to take control and whip people into shape. He never addresses the senior pastor

HE NEVER COMMANDS THEIR ELDERS TO TAKE CONTROL AND WHIP PEOPLE INTO SHAPE. HE NEVER ADDRESSES THE SENIOR PASTOR AT ALL IN THIS LETTER, OR ANY OTHER LETTER. WHY? BECAUSE THERE WASN'T ONE.

at all in this letter, or any other letter. Why? Because there wasn't one.

The overwhelming evidence throughout the New Testament is that every baptized believer in Christ was automatically ordained by the Holy Spirit into the ministry of Jesus. There was no separation between clergy and laity.

Were there some within the Body who were gifted to teach and to encourage and to lead? Yes, of course. But the entire life of the Church did not revolve around these few. Instead, every single believer was empowered to contribute and to speak and to use their gifting as the Holy Spirit directed.

According to the New Testament, when the church actually functions as a real Body, and when Jesus is really the Shepherd, the entire Body will be healthy and operate as God intended all along.

It makes me wonder how can we continually refer to ourselves as "The Body of Christ" if we do not actually engage in the organic form of shared life as described in 1 Corinthians 12.

> "Any system which operates to forbid or render impossible the functioning of every priest according to ability is subversive of God's whole system." (W. Carl Ketcherside[3])

Chances are that, unless you are an ordained pastor, you don't consider yourself as being qualified to baptize a new believer, lead others in the Lord's Supper, or pray for someone dying of cancer in the hospital. If so, you are not alone. Most people who attend Christian churches today would not feel it was their place to baptize a new believer or perform any of the functions normally reserved for the clergy.

The sad thing is, your Bible suggests otherwise. In fact, Paul the Apostle says on several occasions that every member of the Body is competent to lead, to instruct, to exhort and to share.

For example, in Romans 15:14 Paul says, "I myself am convinced, my brethren, that you yourselves are full of goodness, complete in knowledge and competent to instruct one another." In 1 Corinthians 14:31 Paul says, "For you can all prophesy in turn so that everyone may be instructed and encouraged."

This last verse specifies a shared prophetic gifting within the Body, but this shared dynamic is not limited to that specific gifting, especially when compared to what Paul has previously communicated in chapter 12 of this same epistle.

One of the most illuminating verses of scripture in the New Testament which gives us a clear picture of what the original New Testament expression of Church looked like is found in 1 Corinthians 14:26, which says:

> "What then shall we say, brethren? When you come together, everyone has a hymn, or a word of instruction, a revelation, a tongue or an interpretation. All of these must be done for the strengthening of the church."

Here we see a gathering of Believers who all partake of Christ together, sharing their God-given gifts with one another in love for the common good.

The fact is that Jesus gave birth to a Church that was radically different from anything that had ever been known before, or since. It was a Church where every believer was a priest of God and every member was a Temple of His Holy Spirit. The only daily sacrifice was performed by average, everyday people who were filled by the Spirit of the Living God and empowered to live radical lives of love in demonstration of the Gospel message.

THE FACT IS THAT JESUS GAVE BIRTH TO A CHURCH THAT WAS RADICALLY DIFFERENT FROM ANYTHING THAT HAD EVER BEEN KNOWN BEFORE, OR SINCE.

The doctrine of the Priesthood of the Believer is nearly unheard of in today's Churches, and rarely preached on. Mainly,

I would suspect, because for any traditional church to follow through with the implications of this doctrine, many pastors would soon find themselves out of a job. Nevertheless, the New Testament reveals an early Church where everyone participated and shared their spiritual gifts openly with the rest of the Body.

In 1 Corinthians 12:4, Paul says:

> "There are different kinds of gifts, but the same Spirit. There are different kinds of service, but the same Lord. There are different kinds of working, but the same God works all of them in all people."

As we've already pointed out, Paul does not say, "…but the same God works all of them in *one man*." If he did, then we might have a Biblical basis for the all-in-one religious professionals that we currently employ today. Instead, as numerous Biblical Scholars (such as F.F. Bruce, Gordon Fee, and Robert Banks), have clearly remarked, the early Church knew nothing of the clergy class of leader we see today.

Another Biblical Scholar, Howard Snyder, has also said:

> "The clergy-laity dichotomy is a direct carry-over from pre-Reformation Roman Catholicism and a throwback to the Old Testament priesthood. It is one of the principal obstacles to the church effectively being God's agent of the kingdom today because it creates a false idea that only 'holy men,' namely, ordained ministers, are really qualified and responsible for leadership and significant ministry. In the New Testament there are functional distinctions between various kinds of ministries but no hierarchical division between clergy and laity. The New Testament teaches us that the church is a community in which all are gifted and all have ministry."[4]

Biblical Scholar William Bausch, himself a Roman Catholic, also freely admits that the New Testament Church knew nothing of the One-Man-Pastorate that we employ in today's modern Christianity:

"Our survey has shown us that no cultic priesthood is to be found in the New Testament. Yet we wound up importing Old Testament, Levitical forms and imposing them on Christian ministry...Nevertheless in practice there is no denying that there has historically been a gathering into one person and his office what were formerly the gifts of many...[This practice] goes astray, of course, when it translates to mean that only ordination gives competence, authority, and the right of professional governance. It goes further astray when eventually all jurisdictional and administrative powers in the church come to be seen as an extension of the sacramental powers conferred at ordination. In short, there is a movement here away from the more pristine collaborative and mutual ministries of the New Testament."[5]

Whenever someone suggests that it is unbiblical for the average Christian to teach, preach, baptize, or prophesy on a regular basis they are dead wrong. While the New Testament teaches us that not all Christians are specifically gifted as teachers, prophets, or apostles, (see 1 Corinthians 12:29) it also teaches that every Christian is a minister, a functioning priest, and is capable of instructing, prophesying, and exhorting in the church.

The truth is that if you are a spirit-filled child of God then the Holy Spirit living within you has already licensed, ordained and empowered you to begin your ministry as a Priest of God in the Name of Jesus Christ, and the function of the Body is to encourage and equip you to walk out that Divine calling every day of your life. It doesn't take much digging around to uncover a host of Biblical Scholars who freely admit that our modern divide between Clergy and Laity is not a New Testament concept.

As Herbert Haag said:

"In the Catholic Church there are two classes, clergy and laity...This structure does not correspond to what Jesus did and taught. Consequently it has not had a good effect in the history of the Church ...Among his disciples Jesus did not want any distinction of class or rank...In contradiction to this instruction of Jesus, a 'hierarchy,' a 'sacred authority,' was nevertheless formed in the third century."[6]

Jesus was quite clear when he pulled his Disciples aside (many of whom would go on to become the Apostles who would shape the New Testament Church) and said to them:

> "(The Pharisees) do all their deeds to be seen by others...But you are not to be called rabbi, for you have one teacher, and you are all brothers." (Matt. 23:5)

What did Jesus mean by this? Did He seriously intend to communicate that He was the only head of His Church? Could He really mean that they were not to set up a hierarchical system of Church government?

Let's ask ourselves the following questions: Where in the Scriptures can we find anyone other than Christ who is called the head of the Church?

The truth is, Jesus never relinquished control over His Disciples or His Church, to any human being. But, you might ask, didn't Jesus assign anyone to lead the Church in His absence? Yes, He did:

> "But I tell you the truth: It is for your good that I am going away. Unless I go away, the Counselor will not come to you; but if I go, I will send him to you...But when he, the Spirit of truth, comes, he will guide you into all truth. He will not speak on his own; he will speak only what he hears, and he will tell you what is yet to come. He will bring glory to me by taking from what is mine and making it known to you." (John 14:7; 13-15)

Here we see that Jesus did leave someone in charge in His absence—the Holy Spirit. Therefore, Jesus continues to lead His Church today, as His people (the Body) respond to His leadership and submit to Him and to the Holy Spirit.

The practical implications of this teaching suggest that whenever believers in Christ gather together in His name, the author of the Scriptures is in our midst. The central character of the Bible lives within us and He is capable of making His will known to us. I declare to you, with complete confidence, that if you read the Scriptures and ask the Lord to reveal Himself to you and to teach you, He will do it! Here's how I know:

I DECLARE TO YOU, WITH COMPLETE CONFIDENCE, THAT IF YOU READ THE SCRIPTURES AND ASK THE LORD TO REVEAL HIMSELF TO YOU AND TO TEACH YOU, HE WILL DO IT!

> "If any of you lacks wisdom, he should ask God, who gives generously to all without finding fault, and it will be given to him." (James 1:5)

> "As for you, the anointing you received from him remains in you, and you do not need anyone to teach you. But as his anointing teaches you about all things and as that anointing is real, not counterfeit--just as it has taught you, remain in him." (1 John 2:27)

> "For where two or three come together in my name, there am I with them." (Jesus in Matt 18:20)

So, even if the people who have the gift of teaching are not present for one of our gatherings, it is still possible for everyone else in the room to read the Scriptures, and pray, and ask God for wisdom and insight. If they do this they should expect to receive revelation from God Himself through the Holy Spirit.

In this way, the Church is never without a teacher. She has been filled with the Spirit of God, and the head of the Church is in her midst. Jesus has promised that He is the Good Shepherd and that His sheep can hear His voice. (see John 10:14-16)

Is it only the leader who can hear the voice of the Shepherd? Or can everyone hear the voice of their Lord? The New Testament strongly argues in favor of the latter.

Again, this doesn't make everyone in the room a teacher, but everyone in the room does have access to hear The Teacher and share what they learn from Him.

Therefore, it's still possible for everyone in the Body to come together under the Headship of Christ and share the gifts they've received from the Holy Spirit and participate in the life of Jesus together.

WHAT ABOUT LEADERSHIP?

Some have suggested that this radical picture of "every-believer-a-priest" goes too far and leaves us with a leaderless Church founded on anarchy and chaos. However, nothing could be further from the truth.

Every Church requires leadership and God has not left us without it. I believe the New Testament demonstrates a plurality of leadership within the Church because every believer is a priest of God. For example, whenever anyone in our house church is sharing he or she is leading us. It may be a seven year old girl, a twelve year old boy, a forty year old man, or anyone else in the room. This is not the end of leadership, it is sharing leadership among the members of the Body, with an understanding that Christ alone is our true leader.

In a larger sense, Christ is still the leader of His Church, not any one person or persons. He might lead through us as we submit to Him and respond to His Holy Spirit, but it is still Christ who is leading us.

So, what is at stake? Do models really matter? Can't God work through us no matter how we gather or who our leader is? Yes, of course God can, and does, work through any and all means to advance His Kingdom and communicate His Gospel.

But, I would simply ask, if you knew that God had something special in mind from the beginning, and if you could see Biblical evidence for a form of Church that empowered every believer to function and contribute to the health of the Body, wouldn't you at least want to give it a shot?

IF YOU KNEW THAT GOD HAD SOMETHING SPECIAL IN MIND FROM THE BEGINNING, AND IF YOU COULD SEE BIBLICAL EVIDENCE FOR A FORM OF CHURCH THAT EMPOWERED EVERY BELIEVER TO FUNCTION AND CONTRIBUTE TO THE HEALTH OF THE BODY, WOULDN'T YOU AT LEAST WANT TO GIVE IT A SHOT?

If there was a way to enter into the kind of community we read about in the book of Acts, why wouldn't you want to entertain the possibility that it could be within our grasp? Why wouldn't you be willing to surrender anything it took to have a Church like that?

Granted, models in themselves only provide the framework. We can see that even those original Christians who gathered in their homes and operated under the headship of Christ were anything but perfect. On the contrary, they were just as weak and prone to failure as the rest of us. What changes us is Christ, not any model of church or method of worship. However, the fact remains that God clearly communicates in the New Testament that the Church founded by Jesus and the form practiced by the early Christians was in fulfillment of His express purpose and desire to establish a temple not made with human hands, where Christ is the Head and where the people of God share equally in the ministry.

Certainly those of us who have made the decision to gather together in an organic way and step into the priesthood of the believer are in the minority, for now. But according to Leadership Magazine, Christianity Today, Focus on the Family and Rev

Magazine, approximately 1,500 pastors a month leave the traditional pastorate in the United States alone, and a recent Gallop poll showed that 1 million adult Christians per year leave the institutional church in the U.S.—and that number is growing.

I believe that God is up to something. I believe that many of the one million people who leave their pews this year are being lead by the Holy Spirit to enter into a form of Church which Jesus inspired from the beginning, and even now is calling some within His Body to experience today.

As author Reggie McNeal, an authority on church leadership, has said:

> "A growing number of people are leaving the institutional church for a new reason. They are not leaving because they have lost their faith. They are leaving the church to preserve their faith."[7]

GOD'S CHURCH. GOD'S DESIGN.

For far too long men have wrestled with God for control over His people. Jesus modeled a servant leadership style for His disciples, and today many of our leaders emphasize a CEO brand of leadership patterned after the world of big business.

THE APOSTLE PAUL TOLD US THAT WE ARE THE TEMPLE OF THE HOLY SPIRIT, YET MANY MINISTERS TODAY INSIST ON COLLECTING MILLIONS OF DOLLARS FROM THEIR FLOCK TO BUILD A TEMPLE WHERE PEOPLE CAN WORSHIP.

The Apostle Paul told us that we are the Temple of the Holy Spirit, yet many ministers today insist on collecting millions of dollars from their flock to build a temple where people can worship.

The Apostle Peter told us that we are the living stones God is building up to become His Church, and instead we are convinced that building the Church involves filling the pews on Sunday morning.

Jesus commanded us to make disciples, those who would follow His teachings and apply them to their everyday life. Instead we have become experts at entertaining the saints each week and occasionally converting a few to our denomination.

I end this chapter with an eye-opening quote by the great philosopher, Soren Kierkegaard:

> "The matter is quite simple. The Bible is very easy to understand. But we Christians are a bunch of swindlers. We pretend to be unable to understand it because we know very well that the minute we understand it, we are obliged to act accordingly. Take any words in the New Testament and forget everything except pledging yourself to act accordingly. 'My God,' you will say, 'if I do that my whole life will be ruined. How would I ever get on in the world'? Herein lies the real place of Christian scholarship. Christian scholarship is the Church's prodigious invention to defend itself against the Bible, to ensure that we can continue to be good Christians without the Bible coming too close. Oh, priceless scholarship, what would we do without you? Dreadful it is to fall into the hands of the living God. Yes, it is even dreadful to be alone with the New Testament."[8]

Let us be people who put the words of Jesus into practice every day of our lives, by the Grace of God.

ORDINATION IS FOR EVERY BELIEVER

There are some who strongly object to the idea of a special group of clergy class Christians who are ordained into the ministry of the Gospel. However, I think the real sin is that *everyone* who follows Jesus isn't ordained into the ministry.

As W.Carl Ketcherside remarks in his book, *The Royal Priesthood*:

"[In the early Church] those who were Christians did not speak of 'entering the ministry.' They were already in it. Everyone entered the ministry at baptism. To be in Christ was to be in the ministry. No one went away to study for 'the Ministry.' Each one began where he was and announced the Messiah who had come. People did not send for a preacher. They just began preaching. All who had been inducted into the kingdom could tell what they did and why they did it. Every Christian was a minister, everyone was a priest. The congregation was a priesthood—a royal priesthood composed of all believers."

OUR CURRENT MODEL OF ORDINATION IS FLAWED, BUT FOR ME THE FLAW IS NOT THAT CERTAIN MEN ARE ORDAINED, BUT THAT NOT ALL MEN AND WOMEN ARE ORDAINED INTO THE MINISTRY.

Our current model of ordination is flawed, but for me the flaw is not that certain men are ordained, but that *not all* men and women are ordained into the ministry.

Rather than to condemn those who hear God's voice and respond to His calling on their lives to serve others and follow Jesus with their whole life, let's applaud their example and take this practice all the way to the finish line by opening wide the doors to enter the ministry of Jesus.

"Again Jesus said, 'Peace be with you! As the Father has sent me, I am sending you.'" (John 20:21)

Every believer is in the ministry of Christ. Each of us has been called, and sent, and gifted, to love and serve and proclaim the Gospel of the Kingdom to everyone we meet.

This doesn't mean that we are all evangelists, or that we are all church-planters, or that we are all teachers (see 1 Corinthians 12). However, it does mean that we are all part of the Body of Christ and that the Holy Spirit has gifted each of us with an important and necessary set of spiritual gifts. These gifts are meant to be used in proportion to our specific calling. Honestly,

I have been licensed and ordained since I was 22 years old, but these days I wish I didn't have the paper. In the beginning it gave me validation for stepping out under the authority of God, but now I can see that it has also created a false sense of clergy and laity—even in our own house church setting.

For example, when we had our first baptism in our house church family, I was the one who performed it. It didn't even occur to me that by taking that position I was robbing others of the experience we should all feel free to enjoy. Needless to say, I will not do that again, nor will I lead the communion for everyone else, or rule the meeting as if this were my church to do with as I please.

So, are you a Priest in God's House? Yes, you are. Every follower of Jesus is a Missionary—in the sense that each of us "in the ministry." The essential thing for each of us, then, is to discover our mission field (where we live, work, eat and sleep), and to step into our ministry (which is determined by our specific gifting by the Holy Spirit).

Now, for those of you who consider yourselves followers of Jesus, I encourage you to go out into your mission field and to step into your daily ministry, because you and I are all ordained into the ministry of Jesus. We are all filled with the Holy Spirit of the Living God. We are Temples of the Holy Spirit. We are all priests of God. We are all living sacrifices.

> THE ESSENTIAL THING FOR EACH OF US, THEN, IS TO DISCOVER OUR MISSION FIELD (WHERE WE LIVE, WORK, EAT AND SLEEP), AND TO STEP INTO OUR MINISTRY (WHICH IS DETERMINED BY OUR SPECIFIC GIFTING BY THE HOLY SPIRIT).

You have been ordained into the ministry of Jesus, my friends. Let us walk and live and love accordingly.

WHAT THE CHURCH IS

In the next section, I want to talk about what the Church is *not*. But first I think it makes sense for us to spend some time exploring what the Church *really is* according to the New Testament scriptures.

In the writings of Paul we see the Church defined as an organism, or a body, where Christ is the only Head.

> "And God placed all things under his feet and appointed him to be head over everything for *the church, which is his body*, the fullness of him who fills everything in every way." (Eph 1:22-23)

> "For a husband is the head of his wife as Christ is the head of the church. He is the Savior of *his body, the church*." (Eph 5:23)

> "Christ is the head of *the church, which is his body*." (Colossians 1:18)

The New Testament also speaks of the Church as being part of the Family of God where God is our Father and Jesus is both our brother and our Lord.

> "For those who are led by the Spirit of God *are the children of God*." (Romans 8:14)

> "So in Christ Jesus *you are all children of God* through faith." (Galatians 3:26)

> "See what great love the Father has lavished on us, that we should be called *children of God! And that is what we are!*" (1 John 3:1)

The New Testament also refers to the Church as a Bride with Christ as our Bridegroom.

> "Let us rejoice and be glad and give him glory! For the wedding of the Lamb has come, and *his bride has made herself ready.*" (Revelation 19:7)

"'For this reason a man will leave his father and mother and be united to his wife, and the two will become one flesh.' This is a profound mystery— but *I am talking about Christ and the church.*" (Eph. 5:31-32)

As we have already seen many times already, the New Testament also affirms that the Church is a spiritual house and a temple "not made with human hands" with Christ as our chief cornerstone. (See Ephesians 2:21, 1 Peter 2:5, Hebrews 3:6)

We have also explored how the New Testament reveals that the Church is a priesthood of believers who are capable of hearing God's voice and being taught by the Holy Spirit. (See 1 Peter 2:5, Revelation 5:10, John 10:11-14)

Each of these pictures of the Church in the New Testament reveals to us the nature of our identity in Christ. We are invited to take part in an intimate relationship with Christ Jesus Himself. We are His Body. We are His Bride. We are His adopted children. We are interconnected stones being built into a temple in which He lives by His Spirit. We are His priests and His ambassadors. He is our Bridegroom, our Head, our brother and He is our High Priest.

Now that we know what the Church is, let us take a moment to look closely, and honestly, at what the Church is *not*.

WHAT THE CHURCH IS NOT

As we've seen, the New Testament uses several words and metaphors to express the character, function, and personality of the Church. Namely, the Church is a Body, a Bride, a Temple, and a Family.

Now that we've spent time exploring what the Church is, let's take a hard look at what the Church isn't. The New Testament doesn't ever refer to the Church as an organization, as if it were a corporation or an industry. Instead, the Church is referred to as an organism. Therefore, according to the Apostles, and to Jesus, the Church that God designed is not intended to be thought of, or to be treated, like a business.

The Church that God always wanted is a family. This means that pastors are not synonymous with CEOs. It also means that the people in the Church are not to be thought of, or treated, as employees, commodities, tithing units, or assets. Instead, they are our brothers and sisters in Christ and should be treated as such—with love and respect.

SO, I HAVE FOUND THAT, IF YOU THINK OF THE CHURCH AS A BUSINESS YOU WILL BEGIN TO EXPECT CERTAIN THINGS FROM IT THAT YOU WOULDN'T EXPECT FROM A FAMILY, AND VICE VERSA.

This is about more than mere semantics. What you believe about something, how you talk about it, how you think of it, actually affects your behavior towards it or concerning it. So, I have found that, if you think of the Church as a business you will begin to expect certain things from it that you wouldn't expect from a family, and vice versa.

For example, no one expects the family to grow in size each quarter or post an annual profit. Families don't work that way, but corporations do. A father would not treat his daughter like an employee. Nor would he base his relationship on how much revenue she contributed to the family. Corporations may act that way, but families do not.

For a long time now, especially in the West, the Church has turned her gaze to the world of big business. She has based Her identity on a corporation rather than the organic, family-based, relational design laid out for us in Scripture.

Perhaps looking at some definitions will help us to see the difference between an organism and an organization.

ORGANIZATION—(Noun) 1- The act of organizing a business or business-related activity; "he was brought in to supervise the organization of a new department." 2- The activity or result of distributing or disposing persons or things properly or methodically. 3- An ordered manner; orderliness by virtue of being methodical and well organized.

ORGANISM—(Noun) 1- Any biological entity capable of replication or of transferring genetic material. 2- Any living entity that has (or can develop) the ability to act or function independently. 3- A system considered analogous in structure or function to a living body.

Scripture makes it clear to us that the Church is an organism; a living Body made up of living parts which function best when they are interconnected. God's design for His Church is relational.

> "The body is a unit, though it is made up of many parts; and though all its parts are many, they form one body. So it is with Christ." (1 Corinthians 12:12)

A family is a social unit made up of people who share a common ancestor and engage in shared activities and beliefs. The family is grounded in love and it takes strength from the quality of the relationships developed over time.

Healthy families love each other in spite of difficulty, or hurt feelings. Families forgive and share.

Families pull together in a conflict. Families support one another and encourage one another. But when a family is run like a business it is impossible to maintain any of these foundational values of love, loyalty, sharing, forgiveness and protection.

A business is grounded in a completely different set of values. A business is a collection of talented people recruited to advance the interests of the company, build recurring revenue streams and add value to the business.

Whenever an employee becomes unproductive he is eliminated. Whenever a more talented employee is recruited, others are down-sized or let go. A business is ultimately about making money and growing larger. A business is mostly concerned with gaining market share and outperforming the competition.

So, if we treat the House of God like a business we will suddenly find ourselves engaging in activities that serve to grow the business and eliminate the competition.

Ideas such as love and family and service and community may become phrases used as metaphors to describe the activities of our business. They will not be expressed or embodied, in any real way, by those within our organization.

A business is concerned with growth, not with how happy, or healthy the employees may be. A business is concerned with numbers, finances and outward signs of success, it is not concerned with forgiveness, community or love.

BUSINESS—(Noun) 1- A commercial or industrial enterprise and the people who constitute it. 2- The activity of providing goods and services involving financial and commercial and industrial aspects. 3- The principal activity in your life that you do to earn money.

FAMILY—(Noun) 1- A social unit living together. 2- Primary social group; parents and children. 3- People descended from a common ancestor. 4- An association of people who share common beliefs or activities. 5- A person having kinship with another or others.

The people who make up a family are called brothers and sisters. They are treated with love and respect. They are all valued for who they are as people, not for what they can do to improve the bottom line.

The people who make up a business are called employees. They are treated as assets which the company may exploit for financial gain. Employees are regarded as individual components which contribute to the overall success of the business. They are valued for what they can add to the company, not for who they are as people.

EMPLOYEES—(Noun) 1- A worker who is hired to perform a job. 2- The employee contributes labor to an enterprise. Employees perform the discrete activity of economic production. An employee may contribute to the evolution of the enterprise, but usually has little control over the productive infrastructure, such as intellectual property and business contacts. Employees usually are the labor in the three factors of production, the others being land and capital.

BROTHER—(Noun) 1- A male with the same parents as someone else. 2- A male person who is a fellow member of a fraternity or religion or other group). 3- Used as a term of address for those male persons engaged in the same movement.

SISTER—(Noun) 1- A female person who has the same parents as another person. 2- A female person who is a fellow member of a sorority or religion or other group.

ACCORDING TO THE NEW TESTAMENT, GOD'S PLAN WAS FOR HIS PEOPLE TO OPERATE LIKE A FAMILY, WHERE HE IS OUR FATHER.

The Church, as Jesus designed it, is relational and organic. According to the New Testament, God's plan was for His people to operate like a family, where He is our Father. He created a church that operates like an organism where He is our head, not like a business where we set up certain people as CEO's and treat people as employees.

Clearly, the New Testament reveals that the Church is a family, an organism and a Bride. It is never referred to as a business venture.

As we've seen over and over again, the mission of the Messiah was to build a suitable temple for God to dwell in. Jesus alone is the one who is qualified to build the temple of God, and we are that temple. We are a spiritual house of living stones "not made with human hands" but by the nail-scarred hands of God's only son.

Put another way, the only true temple of God is the one that is being built by Jesus, not one built by any man, pastor, teacher or leader.

A FIRST CENTURY PAGAN TALKS TO A FIRST CENTURY CHRISTIAN

Imagine the conversation between an unbelieving Pagan in the first century and a follower of The Way:

Pagan: "I would like to know more about this Christ you speak of. Where is your temple?"

Christian: "We don't have one."

Pagan: "What? Then where does one go to meet with your God?"

Christian: "We are all the Temple of the Holy Spirit, so God meets with us wherever we are."

Pagan: "Hmm...then where do you conduct your sacrifices?"

Christian: "We have no animal sacrifice at all. Jesus became our sacrifice so that we could be free. Our only sacrifices are our own lives as we surrender to Him and His will every day."

Pagan: "Fascinating! I would love to meet your Priest to learn more about this."

Christian: "Well, I am a Priest."

Pagan: "You are?! But I thought you sold pottery in the marketplace? How can you be a Priest in this new religion?"

Christian: "You can be one also if you submit your life to Christ and place your trust in Him. We are all Priests of God."

Wasn't it a radically different system of faith that Jesus gave His life to create? Why has the Church today become an institutionalized religion when it began as something so utterly unique and different that it captured the imagination of the common people and stood apart from the man-made religions of the day?

According to Paul in Ephesians, the Church was created by God to communicate and model something radically different from the systems of this world.

> "His (God's) intent was that now, through the church, the manifold wisdom of God should be made known to the rulers and authorities in the heavenly realms, according to his eternal purpose which he accomplished in Christ Jesus our Lord." (Eph. 3:10-11)

WHY HAS THE CHURCH TODAY BECOME AN INSTITUTIONALIZED RELIGION WHEN IT BEGAN AS SOMETHING SO UTTERLY UNIQUE AND DIFFERENT THAT IT CAPTURED THE IMAGINATION OF THE COMMON PEOPLE AND STOOD APART FROM THE MAN-MADE RELIGIONS OF THE DAY?

The Church was part of God's plan to reveal the mystery of God to the world. That included a variety of areas where the Church would look and behave differently than others around them.

The Church was to be a place where there were no divisions of race, sex, or social status. When Paul says, *"There is neither Jew nor Greek, slave nor free, male nor female, for you are all one in Christ Jesus" (Gal. 3:28)* this is part of what he is trying to communicate. The Church isn't meant to look or act or behave like the world.

It was designed by God to be different and to reflect a Heavenly design, not an earthly, man-made quality.

So, when we take God's organic design based on a family of equals and trade that for a man-made design patterned after the business world, we are denying our

God-inspired DNA and dismantling our intended purpose to reflect the "manifold wisdom of God" by setting ourselves apart from the world.

THE CHARACTER OF THE NEW TESTAMENT CHURCH

The New Testament church did not collect money to be spent on salaries, programs, buildings or itself.

The New Testament church was primarily concerned with making disciples and caring for the poor, the orphan and the widow.

> **THE NEW TESTAMENT CHURCH DID NOT ELECT A SEPARATE "CLERGY CLASS" TO PERFORM SPECIAL RELIGIOUS DUTIES. INSTEAD EVERYONE WAS "IN THE MINISTRY" AND EMPOWERED TO SERVE AND LOVE AS THE SPIRIT WILLED.**

The New Testament church did not elect a separate "clergy class" to perform special religious duties. Instead everyone was "in the ministry" and empowered to serve and love as the Spirit willed.

The New Testament church did not attempt to follow an Old Testament code of worship.

The New Testament church affirmed the priesthood of the believer and allowed every member to share, participate and take an active part in the regular functioning of the church itself. These activities included baptism, sharing communion, preaching the Gospel and making disciples.

The New Testament church did not keep a bank account. Instead it gave away all the funds laid at the Apostles' feet in order to plant churches and care for those in need—both within and without the church body.

The New Testament church leaders were humble servants who waited on tables, washed feet, served others, laid hands on the sick, and encouraged the persecuted.

They understood that true greatness was found at the feet of others, rather than at the top of the ladder.

The New Testament church did not segregate themselves based on age, sex, race, music preference, political affiliation, ethnic background, or any other criteria.

Everyone who named the name of Christ, regardless of age, sex or race, was immediately a fully functional and valued member of the Body of Christ.

The New Testament church did not verbally, politically or physically oppose the oppressive Roman government or pagan religions of the day. Instead they simply lived extravagant lives of love among their neighbors and served anyone in their path as Jesus commanded.

The New Testament church was not in favor of violence, nor did it participate in armed conflict, not even in self-defense. Instead, the early followers of Jesus quietly imitated their Lord and gave up their property, submitted to prison and went to their deaths peacefully.

The New Testament church allowed every member—male or female, slave or free, Jew or Gentile to preach the Gospel, plant churches, teach the Word, and lead worship every single day.

The New Testament church had no one single location where "Church" was located. Worship was not seen as something that happened in a particular location or on a particular day or with the assistance of particular people. Instead, worship was seen as a life continually submitted to Christ as a living sacrifice for the good of others, to the glory of God.

The idea of a "worship service" is completely foreign to the New Testament. The New Testament church understood the

Gospel of the Kingdom to be about God's Kingdom (rule and reign) being released in the heart of every follower of Jesus. It was not something that would come one day after the death of the saints or the return of Christ.

The New Testament church did not consider the work of the Holy Spirit to be weird or strange. Instead they accepted the moving of the Holy Spirit within the Body as the natural and continual ministry of Jesus being released in the Body. To heal, teach, instruct, correct, rebuke, inspire, encourage and empower the people of God was to carry the Gospel of the Kingdom and live a life of love for the sake of others.

> THE NEW TESTAMENT CHURCH DID NOT CONSIDER THE WORK OF THE HOLY SPIRIT TO BE WEIRD OR STRANGE. INSTEAD THEY ACCEPTED THE MOVING OF THE HOLY SPIRIT WITHIN THE BODY AS THE NATURAL AND CONTINUAL MINISTRY OF JESUS BEING RELEASED IN THE BODY.

The New Testament church was always being taught to love one another and to imitate the love of Christ and to humbly serve others as Jesus did. They were not concerned in any way with amassing wealth, gaining status in the community, becoming politically powerful, being respected, changing laws, picketing the funerals of homosexuals, or speaking out against pagan practices. They were not interested in selling products with their church name, cross, or scripture verse attached.

The New Testament church did not have a name. The New Testament church did not brand itself. The New Testament church did not provide a salary or ongoing stipend to those within the Body who functioned as Elders, Overseers, Shepherds, Teachers, or Facilitators. The people who performed these functions within the Body did so out of love and were only compensated by the Holy Spirit with joy.

The New Testament church did not have a pulpit from which sermons were spoken by ordained clergy. The New Testament church did not have a Bible, or even a copy of the entire Old Testament, yet this Body managed to preserve the teachings of Jesus, the doctrines of the faith, the creeds and Gospel of the Kingdom with only the empowering presence of the Holy Spirit, and the teaching of the Apostles to guide them.

The New Testament church did not market itself or the Gospel. Instead the original followers of Jesus concentrated on loving as Jesus loved, giving and sharing as Jesus did, and concerned itself with the welfare of others in need; both inside and outside the Body.

If the world needs anything today, it desperately needs a return of the New Testament form of Church and a New Testament brand of Christianity.

TERTULLIAN'S WINDOW

If you'd like to know what it was like to attend a Christian gathering in the early days of the faith, here's a great look at what they were doing in the 2nd Century according to Tertullian, a second century Christian:

> "We are a society with a common religious feeling, unity of discipline, a common bond of hope. We meet in gatherings and congregations to approach God in prayer, massing our forces to surround Him...We meet to read the divine Scriptures...Our presidents are elders of proved character.

> "Even if there is a treasury of a sort, it is not made up of money paid in initiation fees, as if religion were a matter of contract. Every man once a month brings some modest contribution—or whatever he wishes, and only if he does wish, and if he can; for nobody is compelled; it is a voluntary offering...to feed the

poor and to bury them, for boys and girls who lack property and parents, and then for slaves grown old.

"So we, who are united in mind and soul, have no hesitation about sharing property. All is common among us—except our wives. At that point we dissolve our partnership.

"Our dinner shows its idea in its name; it is called by the Greek name for love (Agape)…We do not take our places at table until we have first partaken of prayer to God. Only so much is eaten as satisfies hunger. After water for the hands come the lights, and then each, from what he knows of the Holy Scriptures, or from his own heart, is called before the rest to sing to God.

"Prayer in like manner ends the banquet…"9

WHO WILL BUILD THE HOUSE?

"Unless the LORD builds the house, its builders labor in vain."

—PSALM 127:1

Whenever I read about a local church raising millions of dollars to build a house where they can worship God it grieves my heart. Why? Because God Himself has already promised to build His house, His Temple. He does not need our help to do this.

WHY ARE WE STILL BUILDING MAN-MADE TEMPLES TO GOD WHEN WE ALREADY HAVE THE SPIRIT OF THE LIVING GOD LIVING WITHIN EACH AND EVERY ONE OF US WHO FOLLOW JESUS CHRIST AS LORD AND SAVIOR?

"And I tell you that you are Peter, and on this rock I will build my church, and the gates of Hades will not overcome it." (Matthew 16:18)

Why are we still building man-made temples to God when we already have the Spirit of the Living God living within each and every one of us who follow Jesus Christ as Lord and Savior? God already commissioned a new temple over two thousand years ago. It was also very costly and was purchased at the expense of God's own Son. On the cross, Jesus destroyed the temple of His Body and fulfilled God's promise to pour out His Spirit on all flesh. God Himself tore the veil in the old temple, even as the foundation was being laid upon the Cornerstone of the New Temple of God.

What's sad to me is that people still believe that they must come each week to a certain place in order to worship and celebrate God. Yet God's design was to expand His worship to cover the earth, and to become a daily, living act of praise and surrender and worship to His amazing and Holy name. Not for one holy day but for every single day of the week.

People do not need a building. They need to know a God who loves them. They do not need an impersonal club to join. They need to be embraced into the loving Family of God. They do not hunger for giant screen televisions and professional sound systems. They are yearning for an intimate relationship with Jesus.

When Jesus had fulfilled the role of the High Priest and offered himself as the final Lamb of God, and the veil in the temple was ripped in half, from top to bottom, He made a way for us, the people of God, to become the new temple, not made with human hands, but spreading out over the whole earth, and living as the new priesthood of believers, to make known His Glory among the nations.

We do not need a temple because we are the temple. We do not need a priest, or a senior pastor, because we are all priests of God, empowered and filled by His Holy Spirit. We do not need an animal sacrifice to be made, because He was our final blood sacrifice, and we are now the living sacrifice, daily dying to ourselves and carrying our cross to follow Him.

Let us not return to the rubble and rebuild the man-made temple. Let us not take up needle and thread and repair the veil that was torn. Let us not commission special priests and clergy who will stand before God in our place.

Our identity, as followers of Jesus, runs deeper than brick and mortar. It transcends a building. It goes beyond ceremony. Our identity as disciples of Christ is defined by a relationship between a Loving God, and a Living Temple made of people who love God, and love others.

You are the temple God has always wanted. He has already bought and paid for us. Let us focus our time and energy on "being the Church," not attending one, or building one out of stone.

SHIFTING MY PARADIGM

The year I was licensed and ordained as a pastor they handed me a key to the church building. I was barely 22 years old, newly married, with a heart full of hope about my calling to pastor God's people.

On Sunday evenings I would unlock the old building an hour early and wander through the dark corridors behind the stage, through the choir room, up through the narrow stairway to the baptistry, quietly talking with God as I moved through the silence of an empty church.

Those were sweet times for me. I remember pouring my heart out to God during those moments, dreaming of the future, wondering where my journey with God would take me, how things would turn out down the road.

Imagine my shock when someone suggested to me that God didn't actually live in that place. He didn't splash in the baptistry when no one was there. He didn't hum His favorite hymns in the darkness waiting for us to return on Sunday morning or

Wednesday evening. He wasn't confined to that place as if it were some Holy container for His Glory.

That idea took me some time to process. I knew in my heart it was true. Scripture even supported the concept that man could not build a house for him, nor did he ever ask for us to construct a castle for his Spirit to dwell. In fact, the only temple God has ever wanted was you and me.

The more this idea permeated my mind, the more revolutionary it became to me. I realized that I could have that same intimate experience with God that I enjoyed in the empty church building on Sunday evenings in my car, or at work, or in the park, or anywhere I went. It was very liberating and empowering for me.

Since we started our house church several years ago, I have had another revelation about the House of God. As we've been hosting church in our living room, our family actually lives in the very place where our church gathers to fellowship and worship.

My own house is now the House of God. I eat in this same house. My family wakes up every single day of the week in this house of worship. We laugh here, we argue here, we cry here, we play here, and we live each day in the same house where the worship and the Bible study and the singing take place every week.

It begins to change the way you think of your house. It starts to affect the way you live. It changes the way you interact with God.

God is not hidden away in a large building somewhere. I do not visit Him each week and catch up on lost time. He does not remain behind when my family leaves to go out to lunch with friends, nor does He sleep on the floor waiting for me to return for Sunday worship.

God has made His home within me. My house is the place where we worship and fellowship each week, but I carry around in my soul the very presence of the living God. Even as I sit at my desk at work, I am on Holy Ground. Even as I pump gas at

MY HOUSE IS THE PLACE
WHERE WE WORSHIP AND
FELLOWSHIP EACH WEEK,
BUT I CARRY AROUND
IN MY SOUL THE VERY
PRESENCE OF THE LIVING
GOD. EVEN AS I SIT AT
MY DESK AT WORK, I
AM ON HOLY GROUND.

the gas station, I am in the presence of the King of the Universe. Even as I sit here, typing this sentence on my computer, sipping my coffee, listening to my favorite music, I am not far from Church.

In fact, I am a member of the Church. God has made His home in me and this is simply a foretaste of the day when I move into His house and eat at His table and we are forever, eternally, together.

What if your house was the House of God? Would it change what you watch on television? Would it affect the way you treat your spouse or your children? Even more, what if the House of God were within your own heart? What if the new ark of the covenant was inside of you? Would it change the things you thought about when no one was watching? This is what the Gospel is all about, isn't it? This is why the scriptures declare:

> "God has chosen to make known among the Gentiles the glorious riches of this mystery, which is Christ in you, the hope of glory." (Col.1:27)

Truth be told, you and I *are* the temple of the Holy Spirit. We are the Body of Christ. We are His hands and His feet. We are His ambassadors. Christ really does make His home within us. Let us celebrate our identity as the household of God and learn what it truly means to "be the Church" rather than merely attend one.

OUT OF BUSINESS

"The God who made the world and everything in it is the Lord of heaven and earth and does not live in temples built by hands."

—ACTS 17:24

I believe it's time the Church went out of business. Close down the bank account, lay off the pastoral staff, cancel the utilities, sell the building, auction off the sound system and the digital projector and turn out the lights.

I know that this is a radical concept, even a scandalous one to most. But it is my firm conviction that the Church needs to get out of the business of being in business because it was never intended by its founder to be run like a business in the first place.

The Church as Jesus imagined it has always been a living organism, not an organization employing a team of spiritual experts. The Church that Jesus died to give birth to isn't a business; it's a family of equals who all love one another in a way the world can only dream of.

If acting like a business prevents us from being the Family God intended, let us joyfully put ourselves out of business and learn what it means to be the Body of Christ in our community. If operating as an organization holds us back from spending time with the neighbors we are commanded to love, then let us resign our pastoral positions and refuse our stipends so that we can share the vibrant love of Jesus with the people living in darkness right next door to us.

Instead of hiring accountants to handle our books, let us join our hands together and walk outside where Jesus always intended His Church to thrive—among the everyday people, the ordinary citizens, the sinners who would never feel at home in our temples.

Instead of investing in state of the art sound systems, let us get down on our knees and wipe the dirt from the faces of the impoverished children who live in our very own cities, just a few miles from our own doorstep, and let us love them as Jesus would have loved them.

Instead of raising millions of dollars to buy a larger building with giant flat-panel television screens in the rotunda, let us give of ourselves, our time, our talent, our energy, our passion and our very best in order to bring the Kingdom of God to a world that so desperately needs hope.

I wonder along with Frederick Buechner, "…if the best thing that could happen to many a church might not be to have its building burn down and to lose all of its money. Then all that the people would have left would be God and each other."[10]

I believe that it's time for the Church to go out of business.

"We in the churches seem unable to rise above the fiscal philosophy which rules the business world; so we introduce into our church finances the psychology of the great secular institutions so familiar to us all and judge a church by its financial report much as we judge a bank or a department store.

"A look into history will quickly convince any interested person that the true church has almost always suffered more from prosperity than from poverty. Her times of greatest spiritual power have usually coincided with her periods of indigence and rejection; with wealth came weakness and backsliding. If this cannot be explained, neither apparently can it be escaped.

"The average church has so established itself organizationally and financially that God is simply not necessary to it. So entrenched is its authority and so stable are the religious habits of its members that God could withdraw Himself completely from it and it could run on for years on its own momentum." (A.W. Tozer[11])

It's time for us to begin to be the Church and not just attend one. I long for the day when we will turn our buildings into a home for runaway girls or forgotten seniors, or a sanctuary for children dying from cancer or AIDs.

I long to break apart the asphalt parking lot and plow it under to grow affordable food for the families living in poverty downtown. I would love to find a way to use these resources for God's Kingdom and for the people He loves enough to die for instead of allowing it to sit empty between services.

I believe that part of what Jesus was doing on the cross was to provide a quality of life for those who would follow after Him. That quality of life is connected to His vision for His Church.

> I BELIEVE THAT PART OF WHAT JESUS WAS DOING ON THE CROSS WAS TO PROVIDE A QUALITY OF LIFE FOR THOSE WHO WOULD FOLLOW AFTER HIM. THAT QUALITY OF LIFE IS CONNECTED TO HIS VISION FOR HIS CHURCH.

He died to create a people who would stop meeting in temples in order to be the living temple of God.

He died to create a people who would stop submitting to the man-made authority of an earthly priest in order to become members of the Priesthood of Believers.

He died to create a people who would stop offering a sacrifice for their sin and start living as sacrifices for the good of others—as loving servants who act as ambassadors of Christ and His Kingdom.

Why would you trade God's vision of Church for the "sermon and a song" we've made it out to be?

I pray that the Church would get out of the business of being a business and start being the Church that Jesus intended us to be all along.

CAN WE IMPROVE ON JESUS?

As someone who makes a living as a copywriter for a large technology distribution company, I'm familiar with big business strategies and the rules of marketing.

Over the years, I've attended seminars and workshops and sat through corporate sponsored tutorials on image, branding, messaging and the ABC's of marketing based on how humans behave, how they react, and what they respond to.

Of course, as I've read and studied and discussed these concepts on a professional level, it's easy to see how someone in the church might want to take advantage of these ideas in order to attract more attendees on Sunday morning. Why not? If we know that people today like this or prefer that, then what's wrong with giving them what they want so that we can grow the church?

Perhaps because, as I have already mentioned, these methods are really all about manipulation. Perhaps it's also because utilizing these methods blurs the actual, intended purpose of the Church itself.

Jesus did not command us to gather large crowds of people. Good Marketing can help you attract and keep a crowd, but that's not what being a Christian, or following Jesus, is all about.

At a conference for Data Capture and Point of Sale vendors and resellers Janet Schijns of Motorola said, *"You cannot achieve tomorrow's results with yesterday's methods."*

From a business perspective this makes sense. Things change and in order to continue to remain profitable it's necessary to keep up with the changing trends and latch onto the most cutting edge technologies available. This works for big biz, but does it work in the Church?

Well, for one thing success in the world of big business is about selling things. It's not about making friends or loving people or serving others or coming alongside the poor or the lonely or the broken. It's not about teaching people how to follow Jesus. Big business defines success as making money, and lots of it, as fast as possible and at the expense of the business down the street from you.

Success in the big business world is about competition. It's about growing your profits. It's about money.

Sadly, the Christian Church in America has decided that success for them is also about competition with the church down the street and about growing larger and making more money. But, if we scan the New Testament we can plainly see that this isn't what Jesus had in mind for His Church.

The major disconnect is that the Church was never meant to be run like a business. The Church, according to the New Testament, is a relational army of servants who give and share and love those around them. It is a family, a bride, an

THE MAJOR DISCONNECT IS THAT THE CHURCH WAS NEVER MEANT TO BE RUN LIKE A BUSINESS.

organism and a body. It is a living, breathing, loving, giving, serving representation of Jesus on this earth.

Was Jesus concerned with competition? Did he affirm his disciples when they chased away someone who was healing in his name, or did he rebuke them for that behavior?

Was Jesus concerned with money? Or did he celebrate both the widow's mite and the harlot's extravagant alabaster expression of love?

Was Jesus concerned with attracting large crowds? Or did he do his best to thin the crowds? Did he retreat to the mountains to be alone? Did he guard his time with his disciples and pour his life into a few?

The quote from Motorola's executive may work for big business, but in the Church if we abandon the example of Jesus and the patterns of the early church in favor of a more business-savvy approach we are in effect improving on Jesus. Is that even possible? Can we improve Jesus?

As a contrast to the quote above let me suggest that if we really hope to enjoy the fruit that the original Christians experienced in the book of Acts we must plant and water and nurture as they did. I would suggest that if we want what they had we will have to do what they did.

Let me respectfully suggest an alternate take on this quote for the church: *"You can't achieve yesterday's results with today's methods."*

Instead I see pastors beating their heads against the wall trying this method or that program to achieve the community and the discipleship and the passion for Christ that they see in the book of Acts. They continually attempt to get what the Acts Christians had without trying to do what they did.

I call this BBQ Waffles because it's like trying to duplicate someone's waffle recipe by reading and following the advice of gourmet BBQ chefs.

Big business executives know how to make money and increase profits and beat the competition.

They do not know how to teach people to love or to serve or to give or to share and they most especially do not know how to teach people how to follow Jesus in their everyday life.

When I look at the early church I am amazed at how they remained committed to Jesus and to His teachings of servant hood, love for others, radical compassion for the poor and non-violence.

It's amazing to me that for over 300 years they continued to hold fast to the example of Jesus who forgave his executioners and prayed for his torturers and went like a lamb to the slaughter. Even when it appeared that it wasn't working, they never gave up on Jesus or His teachings. Even as their property was confiscated they held on tight to the teachings of Jesus. Even when they were thrown to the flames or put to death in the lion's den, they never shrank back from the values of the Kingdom or the Gospel of Christ.

At least, that is, until it appeared that they had won the victory. Once Constantine declared himself to be a Christian and offered them a chance to trade their suffering for leisure and their outcast status for popularity, they blinked. They settled for the best the Empire could give them and they let go of the radical doctrine of Jesus.

Today many who call themselves "Christians" are still unable to let go of their status. They're still unwilling to lay down their considerable resources to embrace the simple teaching of Jesus.

HOW DIFFERENT ARE WE?

The Christians in Acts shared all things. The Christians in Acts sold their possessions and gave it to the poor. The Christians in Acts took their land and their property and liquidated them so that others could be fed and clothed. Their hope was in Jesus alone. Their trust was in the truth of His teachings.

The Church today is afraid of losing Her tax exemption status. The Church today will not sell Her property and give the money to the poor. The Church today does not consider the offering as belonging to the poor but as belonging to the Church. Today's Church is often more concerned about the world of politics than in the conditions of the poor in the community.

Our hope is in our political influence. Our trust is in American Democracy and the power of our vote. I fear that the Church today has become the polar opposite of the Church in Acts. We have become a church that seeks material gain for itself rather than to share with the poor, the outcast, or the outsiders.

Even though following Jesus is a lost art; even though putting his

WE HAVE BECOME A CHURCH THAT SEEKS MATERIAL GAIN FOR ITSELF RATHER THAN TO SHARE WITH THE POOR, THE OUTCAST, OR THE OUTSIDERS.

words into practice may get you into trouble; even though others may criticize you and persecute you for attempting such a thing, I encourage you to follow Jesus today, and every day.

WHAT WAS JESUS LIKE?

- Compassionate

- Loving

- Caring

- Concerned for the poor, the sick, the outcast

- An advocate for peace

- Radically inclusive

- Interested in the lives of others

- Introduced a spiritual solution to our problems

- Comfortable around sinners

WHAT IS THE CHRISTIAN CHURCH LIKE TODAY?

- Intolerant of those who are not like us

- Uncomfortable around sinners

- Concerned for our own personal success

- Not so concerned with the poor, or the outcast

- Focused on political solutions to our problems

- Defined more by what we hate or dislike

- Largely supportive of war against our enemies

YOU ARE THE TEMPLE OF GOD

If we are God's new temple what does that mean? It means we are now the Holy Place. Our bodies—we are now the place where God's Spirit dwells. We carry around with us the immediate presence of God where those who are hungry to meet with Him can come and connect with Him.

YOU ARE THE ROYAL PRIESTHOOD

If you and I are the new priesthood it means that we are the ones who perform the daily sacrifice. We are the ones who are worthy to enter the "Holy of Holies" and approach God. We can hear God's voice. We have the honor of conveying the message of God to those who are outside the Temple. We now play an active role in the spiritual health and education of God's people.

YOU ARE THE DAILY SACRIFICE

If we are the daily, living sacrifice it means each of us have special access to God. Because of His ultimate sacrifice on the cross, our daily sacrifice bears witness to our desire to follow Jesus, surrender our lives to Him, and worship God with our entire being.

UNDERSTANDING WHO YOU ARE

You and I are this same Church. We are the people of God. We are part of something more unique and fabulous than any of us could have ever imagined.

Who are you in Christ? You are a new creation. You are the Temple of God. You are the Priests of God. You are the daily, living sacrifice to God.

We are a people unlike any the world has ever seen or imagined before.

We are the Body of Christ.

EXPLOITATION OR EMPOWERMENT?

Just imagine for a moment that you could be part of a church where the one thing they were extremely good at was to help everyone discover what their calling and gifting was. Then imagine that the one thing they always did next was to set you free and encourage you to follow that dream and live out that God-given calling. Wouldn't that be amazing?

Wouldn't it be incredible to be part of a church that was passionate about helping others realize their hopes and live out their dreams? Can you just imagine how others would speak of a church like that to their friends?

"Do you know what these people did for me? They loved me, they supported me, they encouraged me, they gave me confidence, they cheered me on and they put their resources towards making my life-long purpose a reality."

Wouldn't you want to know how to get to a church like that? Wouldn't you be excited to get in line and have your turn at being empowered and loved and supported and set free to live out the calling and utilize the talents God gave to you?

I just have to wonder, why isn't every Christian Church on the face of the planet like this? Wolfgang Simson, in his book *Houses That Change the World,* put together a fascinating list to help us see the difference between Church as God intended it and Church as we so often experience it:

Give people something to do, or give people something to attend. Believe in people, or make people believe in you. Delegate authority, or require submission to your authority. Further God's plan for their life, or make them part of your plans. Invest in them, or use them. Love them and show it, or love the task more than the people. Give them what you have, or take what they have. Provide resources for growth, or harvest their resources for your own use. Discuss with them, or preach at them. Spend time freely with them, or require appointments that suit your schedule. Give them the keys now, or hold back until you retire. Serve them, or get them to serve you. Praise them, or accept their praise graciously. Transfer master-hood to them, or demonstrate your master-hood to them.[12]

APPLE TREES, NOT JUST APPLES

Someone once pointed out to me that the goal of an apple tree is not to produce more apples. It's to produce more apple trees.

This is the organic purpose found in nature, and it's the organic purpose of the Body of Christ as well.

When an apple tree produces apples that's important. You can't really be an apple tree and not produce apples, of course. But if every-

> SOMEONE ONCE POINTED OUT TO ME THAT THE GOAL OF AN APPLE TREE IS NOT TO PRODUCE MORE APPLES. IT'S TO PRODUCE MORE APPLE TREES.

thing ended there the apple tree would not have achieved the purpose for which God designed it. The apple tree must produce more apple trees in order to realize its full potential. Otherwise, when that tree dies, so does the potential for creating more apples.

In the context of the Christian church I see too many pastors and church leaders who are terrified of taking their brightest and most talented people and releasing them into the world. They feel that losing those gifted, intelligent, talented individuals will somehow make their church poorer and weaker. So they expend a whole lot of energy trying to keep those people busy and connected and plugged in to what they are doing instead of encouraging them to discover their gifting and calling and releasing them to go and to do whatever it is that God has created them for.

A church that practiced encouraging growth like this would be responsible for spawning ministries and providing good fruit for the community on an exponential level. It would also be living out the command of Scripture to seek the good of others around us rather than selfishly seeking our own good (see Philippians 2:3).

Usually the only way someone with talent and vision ever leaves one church to start another is when they leave under protest and start something all by themselves. Why? Because most pastors will tell you that they are not ready to start planting a church until they reach 500 members. The problem with that is when you realize that the average church in America is only about 250 to 300 people. Most never reach the 500 mark, and honestly when they do reach that milestone few of those churches ever actually plant another church because they have not planned to do so.

JUST IMAGINE

Imagine what it would be like if the Church really was a place where everyone was encouraged and empowered and released to live out the calling God has placed on them. I believe that any church that actually lived that out and practiced this sort of extravagant empowerment wouldn't be able to contain the people who flocked to their doorstep. They also wouldn't be able to survive the flood of people unless they were continually sending people out and giving away their brightest and best to fulfill the destiny God had placed on them.

I can't help but feel that this was what Jesus had in mind all along. When he commanded us to love one another and share everything we had with others, Jesus was deputizing us to do the work he started. Jesus trained a handful of men to be salt and light in the world and then he cut them loose and set them free to live out the things he had taught them. He also commanded them to repeat that pattern over and over again. *"Go into the world and make disciples of all nations...teaching them to obey all that I have commanded you..."* he said. And that's exactly what they did. Over and over again.

They followed Jesus and they taught others how to follow Jesus so that they could go out and teach others how to follow Jesus too.

A SCHOOL THAT YOU NEVER GRADUATE FROM

A friend of mine once pointed out that traditional churches today are like schools full of people who will never graduate. Everyone has to sit through essentially the same lecture each week and there is no homework (so the pastor doesn't test who is putting things into practice or not), and worst of all no one ever graduates and becomes an instructor themselves.

A FRIEND OF MINE ONCE POINTED OUT THAT TRADITIONAL CHURCHES TODAY ARE LIKE SCHOOLS FULL OF PEOPLE WHO WILL NEVER GRADUATE.

Here's a great solution: Teach people to become teachers. If you are in the habit of training others to become trainers of others (this is a very basic principle of discipleship), you will eventually end up with a church full of teachers and trainers who are training others to also be teachers and trainers.

RETURN TO THE PRIESTHOOD OF BELIEVERS

Most pastors and on-staff ministers can relate to the fact that only a handful of people do all the work and ministry in the Body while 80% to 90% sit back and do nothing. This creates frustration, burn-out and, honestly, a large group of underdeveloped disciples.

What happened to the Priesthood of the Believer? What happened to opening the Scriptures and trusting the Holy Spirit to lead you into all truth?

> "But you are not like that, for you are a chosen people. You are royal priests, a holy nation, God's very own possession. As a result, you can show others the goodness of God, for he called you out of the darkness into his wonderful light." (1 Peter 2:9)

The liberty offered to us in Christ Jesus was meant to empower every believer to become a committed and devoted disciple who goes and creates other committed and devoted disciples. The early church was not full of seminary trained Bible teachers. Most of those who led the weekly gatherings in their homes were average, ordinary people like you and me. They were led by the Holy Spirit as they prayed, studied the Scriptures and met together with other followers of Jesus each week.

In my experience within the house church I can testify to the truth of the Scriptures where God promises that He will build His church. He doesn't need our help.

He is also true to His word and promise that the Holy Spirit will lead us into all Truth (John 16:13; 1 Cor 12)

THE POWER OF LETTING GO

We have a tendency in our traditional churches to centralize certain people as leaders and, in turn, we disqualify everyone else from participating. I believe that this is not the way God intended things to be. We were not saved and filled with the Holy Spirit to simply remain spectators as a select few act out their calling and live out their purpose.

Each of us in the Body of Christ has a specific calling and gift. If we are not set free to use it as God intended not only will we suffer as individuals, we will suffer as a Body, and the nation will suffer due to our unrealized potential.

Let me encourage you to discover your calling as a valued member of God's Family. Once you've heard God's voice and you've understood the purpose God has for you as an agent of change within this culture, let me be the first to urge you to step outside the nest and spread your wings.

If you feel called to start a Bible Study in your home, do it. If you feel called to go out into the streets and reach out to the homeless, or to the prostitute, go for it. If you have a passion to start a new kind of church that facilitates community and reaches a new generation, make it so.

Don't allow anyone to hold you back. The Kingdom is wide open. Take that first leap...and soar!

PRACTICING CHRISTIANITY

According to the New Testament, the Christian faith was inaugurated at Pentecost when the Holy Spirit, in fulfillment of Joel 2:28-32, was poured out on all flesh. From that day forward, the followers of Jesus became empowered to preach the Gospel, baptize new believers, plant churches, and share communion with other believers. Every follower was in the ministry of Jesus Christ. There was no distinction between clergy and laity because in their minds, every follower of Jesus was "...being built into a spiritual house to be a holy priesthood, offering spiritual sacrifices acceptable to God through Jesus Christ." (1 Peter 2:5)

When the Spirit of Almighty God was poured out on all flesh at Pentecost, those first Christians got it. They understood that the same Holy Spirit of God that once rested over the ark of the covenant behind a 300 pound veil in the Temple of Jerusalem was now living within their own hearts. They were excited beyond belief and consumed with a fire and a passion to share this living presence of God with everyone they knew.

The original Christian church was one "not made with human hands." Rather than following "the pattern of this world" the Biblical Christian church was birthed by the Spirit of God, empowered by the words of Christ, and under submission to the Father. Simply put, the Christian church we read about in the New Testament was something that God was doing, not men. In contrast to our Church today, the first Christians were ordained by the Holy Spirit of God Himself and sent out to proclaim the Gospel, the Good News, that the Kingdom of God had come to every man, woman and child.

The artificial, man-made hierarchy we see in the Christian church today is not what the Church practiced under the Apostles in the New Testament. Unfortunately, over time, the Christian church surrendered the Spirit-filled approach where everyone contributed for a more top-down approach. Of course, as we've already seen, Jesus hoped to inspire a movement where men and women were all empowered by the Holy Spirit to be functioning priests in the Body.

I BELIEVE THIS IS PARTLY WHY JESUS STRATEGICALLY CHOSE HIS DISCIPLES FROM AMONG THE MOST COMMON AND ORDINARY STRATA OF SOCIETY.

I believe this is partly why Jesus strategically chose his disciples from among the most common and ordinary strata of society. He wanted to make sure that when a run-of-the-mill fisherman stood up and proclaimed the Gospel no one would bow down and worship him. Instead, the people saw ordinary men and women just like themselves—uneducated, dirty, and painfully normal people -who had been caught up into the eternal purpose of God.

When Peter spoke under the power of the Holy Spirit, or when Paul prayed for people to be healed, or when any of those unnamed disciples ministered to one another in the Body, everyone knew it was God doing the work, not the people themselves.

> "When they saw the courage of Peter and John and realized that they were unschooled, ordinary men, they were astonished and they took note that these men had been with Jesus." (Acts 4:13)

When they gathered together it wasn't to hear words of "eloquence or superior wisdom" but to experience Jesus in their midst as the Head of the Body and to share Him through a communion that went beyond bread and wine. The original, New Testament Christians were empowered, "not with wise and persuasive words, but with a demonstration of the Spirit's power" (1 Cor.2:1-5)

The Church is what God is doing, not what we are doing. We are living stones, but only because we are filled with the Life of Christ

THE CHURCH IS WHAT GOD IS DOING, NOT WHAT WE ARE DOING.

by the power of the Holy Spirit. Gathering apart from that is just a gathering. When we come together, to the Living Stone, we also like living stones are built up into a holy priesthood, offering sacrifices of praise to celebrate our Risen Lord who is present with us in the meeting.

Can you imagine being in a room with Jesus and allowing someone other than Him to speak for over an hour? Can you imagine experiencing the awesome presence of the Spirit of the

Living God and reading announcements? Clearly, if we actually believed that Jesus was in our midst when we came together as a church, our response would be radically different than what we've come to expect as normative Christianity.

The Body of Christ is an expression of the tangible, resurrected Christ. Have we settled for less? Have we become comfortable listening to the wisdom of men rather than waiting quietly for the whisper of our Eternal Creator?

The more I read the New Testament the more I see a people who were caught up in something beyond themselves. They were the most common, uneducated, normal people you can imagine. Even their leaders were humble, ordinary, everyday men and women who saw themselves as fortunate participants in the fulfillment of Biblical prophecy and the heart's desire of Almighty God to reveal Himself to the World.

GOD'S RELATIONAL CHURCH

"The purpose of the Christian meeting was to hold the common meal, and to make it a memorial of Jesus' Last Supper with the disciples... The exercise of the spiritual gifts was thus the characteristic element in primitive worship. Those gifts might vary in their nature and degree according to the capacity of each individual, but they were bestowed on all and room was allowed in the service for the participation of all who were present. Every member was expected to contribute something of his own to the common worship... Worship in those first days was independent of all forms."

—ERNEST F. SCOTT[13]

It is not God's plan for us to be alone. He has designed His Church to operate as a Family, and as a Body, where each part depends upon the others.

Whenever Satan wants to attack one of us, he always starts by isolating us from the rest of the Body of Christ. Our Enemy knows that if he can separate us from the Body, he can cut off our source of strength, encouragement, love, and the rest of those God designed us to be in fellowship with. It's very true: United we stand. Divided we fall.

> "Let us not give up meeting together, as some are in the habit of doing, but let us encourage one another—and all the more as you see the Day approaching." (Hebrews 10:25)

WE NEED EACH OTHER

God has purposely designed His Church to be interdependent and connected at the molecular level. We've each been given different gifts for the purpose of helping one another to grow to maturity in Christ. Each of us has a spiritual gift (yes, even you) and it only works when we use it for the benefit of others within the Body.

The early church did not resemble what we experience today. The weekly gathering was in a home, meals were shared, everyone contributed and there was no visible leader in the group who did all the talking or teaching while the rest of them listened.

According to 1 Corinthians 12, God has designed His Church to act relationally. He has given everything the Body needs to function and grow to the members of the Body itself, "for the common good." The Body is able to thrive through the power and indwelling of the Holy Spirit, which lives within each member of this Body.

If you read 1 Corinthians 12 and elsewhere in the New Testament, you will not see any teaching or practice within the Body of Christ where all of the gifts flow from one elect leader to everyone else so that they can grow, mature, receive mercy, etc.

What God did do was to give all of the gifts to various people distributed throughout the Body.

In God's relational design for His Church, the encouragement you need is available from someone else in the Body. This means you need the rest of us. It means we need you. We need each other to grow and mature.

Couldn't God have given each person the spiritual gift they needed, when they needed it? Yes, of course He could have. But then we wouldn't need to relate to one another.

Instead, God's plan was to place the gift you need most in the hands of someone else so that you and I are required to communicate our needs with one another. It is necessary for the life and health of the Body that we share our weakness and that we share the gifts we have been given.

> "Just as each of us has one body with many members, and these members do not all have the same function, so in Christ we who are many form one body, and each member belongs to all the others." (Rom.12: 4-5)

We belong to one another. We need each other. We cannot survive alone.

WHOSE WILL BE DONE?

I've counseled several people over the years who have been wounded by someone in the Body, or fallen into a pattern of sin, or given in to depression. In each case they often feel that they must retreat from the Body in order to heal, or to think, or to "take a break" from Church.

Whenever we do this we are allowing ourselves to play into Satan's hand. Our enemy knows that if he can isolate us from the rest of the Body (which was designed by God to strengthen us and build us up in our faith), he has already won the battle.

We need one another. We were designed by God to love and to help and to serve and strengthen one another. If we remove ourselves from fellowship I have to ask, "Whose will is being done?" Certainly not God's will.

If you find yourself in a place where you're drawing away from the rest of the Body of Christ, you need to remember that you belong to Jesus and it's time to return to fellowship in obedience to His Love for you.

KNOWING AND BEING KNOWN

Sometimes people in the Body of Christ will hop around from place to place and church to church, visiting here one week and there the next week. By doing this they avoid accountability and embrace anonymity which is just as dangerous as staying home completely.

Again, God designed the Body to be relational. If we refuse to allow others to know us, if we avoid intimacy in the Body of Christ, we are denying our own spiritual DNA as members of God's Family. When we embrace anonymity we are opening the door for the enemy to draw us away from God and His people.

A good friend of mine shared that his house church family was actively learning to see everything as an opportunity to learn how to love God and love others, or how to receive love from God and receive love from others.

> IF WE REFUSE TO ALLOW OTHERS TO KNOW US, IF WE AVOID INTIMACY IN THE BODY OF CHRIST, WE ARE DENYING OUR OWN SPIRITUAL DNA AS MEMBERS OF GOD'S FAMILY.

God designed His Church, (that's you and I), to operate best when we are sharing openly and loving one another intimately. We can't do that if no one knows us—our pain, our doubts, our hopes, our fears, our dreams, our joys, our sadness, our tears. We have to learn to love others, and to be loved by others, and by God, in all that we do.

In our modern day traditional American church we have abandoned a relational, family structure and embraced a corporate, business model for the Church. We have shifted to an organizational model and not an organism model.

In the words of author and theologian W. Carl Ketcherside:

"We are not left to test and experiment with other forms and ideas. God has established a system which is the climax of all his creative genius. The inferior priesthood of the past pointed toward this sublime age of universal priesthood. We are not to go back to the literal and limited ministry of the previous dispensation, but we are to implement and utilize the spiritual and comprehensive priesthood made possible by the one who first became both sacrifice and priest. God's plan will work for us, if we will work his plan for him."[14]

Do models matter? Yes, they do. If you attempted to run your family like a business it would change the dynamic of your family. Decisions would be made to benefit the business first and the concept of family would become lost in the new corporate structure of your home.

God's design for His Church is important. If we are dying for community it's because we've abandoned a relational form of Church. If we see our pastors burn out and fall away it's because we've twisted God's relational plan for His Church into a one-man show. If our churches are unfriendly and cold it's because we have forsaken a family approach and embraced a corporate structure.

If we're really interested in following Scripture, it's important for us to listen to what it says, and to put these things into practice.

"INCREASING INSTITUTIONALISM IS THE CLEAREST MARK OF EARLY CATHOLICISM—WHEN CHURCH BECOMES INCREASINGLY IDENTIFIED WITH INSTITUTION, WHEN AUTHORITY BECOMES INCREASINGLY COTERMINOUS WITH OFFICE, WHEN A BASIC DISTINCTION BETWEEN CLERGY AND LAITY BECOMES INCREASINGLY SELF-EVIDENT, WHEN GRACE BECOMES INCREASINGLY NARROWED TO WELL-DEFINED RITUAL ACTS...SUCH FEATURES WERE ABSENT FROM FIRST GENERATION CHRISTIANITY, THOUGH IN THE SECOND GENERATION THE PICTURE WAS BEGINNING TO CHANGE."

—JAMES D.G. DUNN

CHAPTER 2

SOME THOUGHTS ON NEW TESTAMENT LEADERSHIP

MERELY FOLLOWERS

"(The Pharisees) do all their deeds to be seen by others…and they love the place of honor at feasts and the best seats in the synagogues and greetings in the marketplaces and being called rabbi by others," Jesus said to his disciples. *"But you are not to be called rabbi, for you have one teacher, and you are all brothers."*

—MATT 23: 5

These instructions from our Lord Jesus are all but forgotten in today's Church. The organizations that dot the fruited plains with His name over the door have not followed the advice of their founder when it comes to leadership.

In fact, not only do we have numerous "rabbis" and "teachers" clogging the airwaves and bookshelves in our modern version of Christendom, we have also become obsessed with the concept of leadership in the Church. We have Leadership Conferences and Leadership Study Bibles and Leadership sections in our bookstores—all devoted to making us better leaders.

With all this special attention placed on leadership and raising up leaders, it's almost as if we're doing all we can to avoid the idea of being merely a follower. Our obsession with leadership suggests to everyone that to be a follower is to be pathetically average. To be a follower is to be lazy. Only those who lack ambition are just followers. It's only the serious Christians who desire to be successful and to be successful in the Body of Christ means being identified as a person with leadership skills and the potential to lead others.

IF OUR DESIRE TO LEAD IS BASED ON THE IDEA THAT WE'RE A BETTER SPEAKER OR TEACHER THAN SOMEONE ELSE, OR IF IT'S BASED ON THE FEELING WE GET WHEN PEOPLE TREAT US LIKE LEADERS, THEN WE'RE IN LEADERSHIP FOR THE WRONG REASONS.

In our lust for position as leaders we've convinced ourselves that being a leader is part of fulfilling our command to make disciples and preach the Gospel to every creature. Yet we cannot truly make a disciple (a follower) unless we ourselves are also disciples and followers of Jesus. This means we must first become devoted to the idea of humbling ourselves daily, taking up our cross, and following Jesus before we dare to instruct someone else in this path.

If our desire to lead is based on the idea that we're a better speaker or teacher than someone else, or if it's based on the feeling we get when people treat us like leaders, then we're in leadership for the wrong reasons.

I can remember being at Pastor's conferences where the idea of being seen as a great leader in the eyes of all the other great leaders was the only thing on anyone's mind, including my own.

All the posturing, the off-hand remarks about the size of my church or the casual references to the innovative approach we were taking to ministry were all calculated to raise my stature in the eyes of the other pastors in the room.

It didn't seem so bad to me at the time because everyone else was behaving the same way. Today I realize there's more to leadership than being perceived as the one with all the answers and I fully repent of this self-centered pursuit of man's approval.

Our ultimate model for leadership is Jesus. He demonstrated a leadership style that flies in the face of our popular ideas of what it means to be a leader. Jesus laid aside his great authority and power and humbled himself from the very beginning, taking on the role of a servant, making himself nothing. Our attitude should be the same. (See Philippians chapter 2).

Even in the House Church Movement we have started to fall into this leadership-centric mindset with authors and experts being sought after to speak at large conferences around the country. We're beginning to create our very own house church celebrities now, and this troubles me. If there's anything our movement can contribute to the Church as a whole it's the concept that everyone matters, not just the leaders among us who instruct and guide us.

Jesus was the one who told his disciples that the one who wants to be the leader has to be willing to wash feet, and serve others and above all to put the needs of others ahead of their own.

> "The greatest among you shall be your servant," Jesus said. "Whoever exalts himself will be humbled, and whoever humbles himself will be exalted." (Matt 23:5-12)

It may not be popular to merely follow Jesus today, but it's the main thing each of us is called to be—a humble follower of Jesus who teaches others how to humbly follow Jesus too.

WHERE ARE THE PASTORS?

Where are all the Pastors in the New Testament? Why are they absent if they are so crucial to the life of the Body? Why is the

WHERE ARE ALL THE PASTORS IN THE NEW TESTAMENT? WHY ARE THEY ABSENT IF THEY ARE SO CRUCIAL TO THE LIFE OF THE BODY? word only used once in the entire New Testament? Why are no letters addressed to them from the Apostles? Why are the Elders (plural) the main form of leadership we see in the New Testament? What were the qualifications necessary to be an Elder or an Overseer? What do these words even mean?

First of all, there is no direct correlation in the New Testament to our modern pastors. None. The word only appears once in the New Testament and it is never unpacked adequately for us to understand exactly what a pastor did. However we can extrapolate based on the root of the word which means "to shepherd." Therefore, pastors were to shepherd the flock and care for them, spiritually. Beyond that we have no other instructions regarding a pastor.

Make no mistake, the leaders of the early church were not the pastors. The most common of all of the New Testament references to leaders are either "elders" or "overseers" and the two are used almost interchangeably throughout the epistles. The term "elders" applies to those who were "old" or "mature." Essentially they were to be followed because they were wise and they deserved respect. The "overseers" were simply those who helped to "oversee" or "facilitate" the gatherings of believers.

From what we see in the New Testament, every church had more than one elder and numerous overseers who helped to guide the church and lead them to follow Christ.

It's fascinating to me that the letters to the Churches in the New Testament are never addressed to the leaders directly, but instead to the Church as a whole.

Certainly there are a few exceptions. Some letters are written directly to people like Timothy or Philemon.

Although many pastors assume that Timothy is an example of a Biblical pastor, in actuality Timothy was engaged in work similar to that of Paul who was busy travelling and preaching the Gospel and planting churches. Timothy is told by Paul to "do the work of an evangelist"—not a pastor. Timothy certainly didn't stay in one place and teach the same people week after week, except in this one case where Paul asked him to do so. Therefore, Timothy is an example of an evangelist or apostle, not a pastor as we might know one today.

The church in Corinth is a fascinating example of a church with numerous moral and ethical failures, yet when Paul writes to correct them he doesn't address their pastor and command him to fix things. In fact, he doesn't even address their elders or overseers to respond to this by exercising their authority over the people. Why were the pastors, or for that matter the elders of the church, not commanded to exercise their authority and deal with the very serious moral failures within the Church in Corinth? Perhaps because Paul understood that the Body itself was capable of coming together to correct the problem themselves. Something he hints at when he says, *"Do you not know that we will judge angels? How much more matters of this life?" (1 Corinthians 6:3)*

A DIFFERENT KIND OF SUBMISSION

I would like to humbly suggest that "Authority", and "Submission" do not necessarily imply organizational structures are at work in the New Testament Church.

Submission is something that all believers are urged to do, and authority is only to be submitted to if it is in line with Scripture and not on the basis of an office or appointment. *"Submit to one another out of reverence for Christ." (Ephesians 5:21)*

Everyone is urged to submit to everyone else. It's a shared submission among brothers and sisters in Christ who are equals

EVERYONE IS URGED TO SUBMIT TO EVERYONE ELSE. IT'S A SHARED SUBMISSION AMONG BROTHERS AND SISTERS IN CHRIST WHO ARE EQUALS AND WHO HUMBLY CARE FOR ONE ANOTHER. ONLY CHRIST IS THE HEAD, OR THE LEADER, OF THE CHURCH.

and who humbly care for one another. Only Christ is the head, or the leader, of the Church.

Many are of the opinion that Jesus actually taught and promoted hierarchy in the Church, something I find alarming and dangerous. But, just for a moment, let me ask, "What would we expect to see in the New Testament if Jesus *didn't* want His Church to be run like a hierarchy?" Wouldn't we expect to see Jesus condemning this practice? Perhaps he would have pointed to a hierarchical system and commanded His disciples not to follow that example?

> "Jesus called them together and said, 'You know that those who are regarded as rulers of the Gentiles lord it over them, and their high officials exercise authority over them. Not so with you. Instead, whoever wants to become great among you must be your servant, and whoever wants to be first must be slave of all. For even the Son of Man did not come to be served, but to serve, and to give his life as a ransom for many.'" (Mk.10:42-45)

Does Jesus command his disciples not to exercise authority over people? Yes, he clearly and plainly does. What, then, are today's pastors doing if they are not exercising their authority over their church members? Isn't this a fair question to ask? Am I allowed to point out the disconnect between what Jesus says and what His Church actually does, or does not, do?

Here, in the Gospel of Mark, Jesus points to the Roman Government (a secular hierarchy) and commands his disciples not to imitate this system of lording it over people or exercising authority over those who follow.

In the Gospel of Matthew, Jesus points to a religious system of hierarchy and instructs them (again) not to imitate this system of hierarchy where the "Teacher" is exalted over the student. Instead, he says, remember that you are all brethren:

> "But you are not to be called 'Rabbi,' for you have only one Master and you are all brothers. And do not call anyone on earth 'father,' for you have one Father, and he is in heaven. Nor are you to be called 'teacher,' for you have one Teacher, the Christ. The greatest among you will be your servant. For whoever exalts himself will be humbled, and whoever humbles himself will be exalted." (Matt. 23:8-12)

Next, let's look at the Apostles themselves. If they heard Jesus commanding them to avoid the hierarchical system of leadership, wouldn't we see evidence that they obeyed this command? Did they take his words to heart? Let's see:

> "Not that we lord it over your faith, but we work with you for your joy, because it is by faith you stand firm." (2 Cor.1:24)

Paul the Apostle obeys Jesus and refuses to "lord it over" those who follow Christ alongside him. Instead he works with them, as a brother, not as an authority figure.

> "To the elders among you, I appeal as a fellow elder, a witness of Christ's sufferings and one who also will share in the glory to be revealed: Be shepherds of God's flock that is under your care, serving as overseers—not because you must, but because you are willing, as God wants you to be; not greedy for money, but eager to serve; not lording it over those entrusted to you, but being examples to the flock. And when the Chief Shepherd appears, you will receive the crown of glory that will never fade away."(1 Peter 5:1-4)

Here, Peter identifies himself, not as an Apostle, but as a fellow elder among the brethren. He then urges these elders (plural) to serve as overseers because they are willing, not because they have been handed a title or an appointment, and especially urges them to be careful not to "lord it over those entrusted to you, but being examples to the flock"—as Jesus commanded him several years earlier.

Having said all of this, doesn't the New Testament ask that we submit to our leaders? Yes, it does. For example:

> "Obey your leaders and submit to their authority. They keep watch over you as men who must give an account. Obey them so that their work will be a joy, not a burden, for that would be of no advantage to you." (Hebrews 13: 17)

This passage in Hebrews above suffers from a horrible translation of the original Greek. The word "authority" is not in the text. "Let yourself be persuaded by your leaders" is a better wording of the passage. Therefore, we are to be submissive to the humble, Godly leadership of those within the Body as it is applied for our spiritual edification and development.

Let me be clear, I am not arguing against leadership here. Not at all. Every church needs leadership, and this is also clearly taught in the New Testament. However I would like to ask us to consider the possibility that leadership doesn't automatically mean top-down, authoritarianism. Jesus modeled something different than this, and then he commanded his disciples to emulate his example.

So, going back to our verse above, you might read this and ask, "What is the basis for our submission to our leaders?" Does their authority rest in the office they hold, or is it found in something else? Are we to submit to these leaders only because they hold an office? Or are we to submit to them as they point us to follow Christ?

Hopefully we do not blindly follow people because they are "the Pastor" or because they have a title of authority. No, the only authority we are to submit to is Christ Himself. To me, this truth is self-evident when we look at the New Testament as a whole. Earlier in this same chapter, the writer of Hebrews, in chapter 13 and verse 7 says, *"Remember your leaders, who spoke the word of God to you. Consider the outcome of their way of life and imitate their faith."*

Here we are told to submit to our leaders as they speak the Word of God to us. Not to them as authorities in and of themselves, but as humble servants who lovingly teach us to follow Christ, and who then demonstrate this by their actual lives of faith.

Submission then is to Christ, who *is* the Word of God. If our leaders handle and teach the Scriptures wisely, and if they faithfully live lives that reflect Christ, *then* we are to submit to their instruction. But only if. Submission is not based on any authority held by one in an office or position. Otherwise, we would be accountable to obey leaders simply because they held that office, regardless of whether or not their lives reflected Christ or their teaching of Scripture was true.

If we follow the policy of hierarchy for the sake of itself we can end up with someone holding an office within the Church and exercising authority even if they are not followers of Christ. Such a person should have no actual authority in any spiritual sense over the life of believers. What counts is character, not the office or the position. However, someone with no organizational office may, because of gifting by the Holy Spirit and sincere love for others,

> IF WE FOLLOW THE POLICY OF HIERARCHY FOR THE SAKE OF ITSELF WE CAN END UP WITH SOMEONE HOLDING AN OFFICE WITHIN THE CHURCH AND EXERCISING AUTHORITY EVEN IF THEY ARE NOT FOLLOWERS OF CHRIST.

have actual authority to speak and teach and lead his brothers and sisters in Christ (who are his equals).

Institutional Churches that employ a man-made organizational method can only hope to mimic the kind of leadership such as the "rulers of the gentiles" possess, something that Jesus expressly commanded us not to do, saying *"It shall not be so among you!" (Matthew 20:25-26)* The Holy Spirit is the only source of spiritual authority and accountability in the Church through real-life relationships, not titles handed down by men.

Did the Apostles depend upon the authority of men or did they give any weight to the opinions of men? Apparently they did not. For example, Paul says, *"Are we beginning to commend ourselves again? Or do we need, like some people, letters of recommendation to you or from you? You yourselves are our letter, written on our* hearts, known and read by everybody." (2 Cor. 3:1-2)

If hierarchy was so important in the early church, why don't we see them exercising it? Why do we see them operating as a Body and not as a business?

Perhaps the answers are right in front of us? Are we courageous enough to answer truthfully?

Richard Halverson famously said:

> "When the Greeks got the Gospel, they turned it into a philosophy; when the Romans got it, they turned it into a government; when the Europeans got it, they turned it into a culture; and when the Americans got it, they turned it into a business."[1]

I pray that God's people would see that they were never intended to be run like a business, and instead that, according to the Scriptures, they are simply a Family, a Body, an Organism, and a Bride.

WHAT IS AN APOSTLE?

As I've been studying the early church the question came to me, "Where did the word 'Apostle' come from?" Looking at the New Testament the word simply appears out of nowhere as the twelve disciples are suddenly, without explanation, referred to as apostles. I started to wonder, "What was the origin of this word? What did it mean to those first century followers of Jesus who heard the word? Was it foreign or strange to them? Did it carry the same meaning for them that it does for us today?"

The word "Apostle" comes from the Ancient Greek, "*apostolos*," which is translated as "someone sent out," or "missionary."

According to Walter Bauer's Greek-English Lexicon of the NT: "Judaism had an office known as apostle." The Friberg Greek Lexicon gives a broad definition as one who is sent on a mission, a commissioned representative of a congregation, a messenger for God, a person who has the special task of founding and establishing churches. The UBS Greek Dictionary also describes an apostle broadly as a "messenger."

With this we can understand a little more about how the early church viewed the apostles. They were church-planting missionaries who preached the Gospel of the Kingdom and continued the ministry of Jesus, the Messiah.

When we look at the New Testament we see plenty of evidence to support this. Peter, James, John, Paul and the other apostles were primarily concerned with traveling to share the Gospel, plant churches and establish a framework for what it meant to be a follower of Jesus.

Christians today seem to hold the apostolic gifting as one above and beyond the common persons of Christendom. Many even go so far as to suggest that there are no apostles in today's church, which is to say that there are no longer church planters or missionaries who are called by God to evangelize the nations and establish the Church of God in the community.

When we read passages like Ephesians 4, verse 11-13 with this in mind it should give us a new perspective on the term "apostle" and the way the early church thought of these people within the Body itself:

> "It was he (Jesus) who gave some to be apostles, some to be prophets, some to be evangelists, and some to be pastors and teachers, to prepare God's people for works of service, so that the body of Christ may be built up until we all reach unity in the faith and in the knowledge of the Son of God and become mature, attaining to the whole measure of the fullness of Christ."

Apostles (church-planting missionaries) were necessary to communicate the Gospel of the Kingdom and establish the Church in Jerusalem, and Samaria, and the uttermost parts of the Earth. They were "first" in a chronological sense because, unless there is someone to go out and preach the Gospel and do the work of an evangelist or missionary, the Church couldn't be established. Once the Gospel is preached, people respond, groups are formed and the Church is established within a community, *then* the Holy Spirit provides for some to become their teachers, their shepherds, and to do the works of service.

NOT A HIERARCHY

I've spent a lot of energy defending the idea that the early church had no hierarchical form of leadership as we know it today. As we begin to see a more practical image of an apostle as a church-planting missionary, this further solidifies the assertion that hierarchy wasn't part of the original Christian experience.

This is why we see Jesus commanding the disciples (and future apostles) not to be like the secular Romans or the religious

Pharisees who love to "lord it over" their followers. Instead, Jesus both commanded and modeled a bottom-up form of servant leadership, not a top-down form of CEO leadership.

MORE THAN 12 APOSTLES

Another surprising discovery in the New Testament is that the apostles are not limited to just "The Twelve" we usually hear about on Sunday morning. These additional Apostles (or "Missionary Church-planters") include Barnabas (Acts 14:14), Andronicus and Junia (Romans 16:7), Silas and Timothy (I Thessalonians 1:1; 2:6, Acts 15:40), and Apollos (1Corinthians 4:6; 4:9; 3:22; 3:4-6).

It's quite fascinating also to consider that many scholars confirm the strongest evidence that the apostle Junia was female (see Romans 16:7) which gives further weight to the idea that the apostolic gifting was simply about doing missionary work and planting churches, not about authority or hierarchy.

Even more interesting is that Jesus himself is named among the apostles in Hebrews 3:1 where he is referred to as the *"apostle and high priest of our professed faith."* In this passage Jesus is identified as the first missionary church-planter who called the twelve disciples to follow him so that he could teach them to be "fishers of men."

While there is a special and unique connection between the original twelve disciples who walked and talked with Jesus personally, and even Paul who encountered the risen Christ in a vision, the actual functional position of an apostle is no more important or special than any other spiritual gift or function within the Body.

The Apostles were very simply and practically the ones who did the work of missionary evangelism and planted churches, and God is still calling His people to be missionaries into the community and plant churches that interact with the culture.

Apostolic succession, then, is simply a continuation of the traditional preaching of the Gospel of the Kingdom, making disciples, planting churches within the community and raising up others who will continually do the same.

THE MYTH OF THE PASTORAL EPISTLES

The letters of Paul to Timothy, and the book of Titus (and sometimes Philemon) are commonly referred to as the Pastoral Epistles of Paul the Apostle. Never mind that these are not written to Pastors. Never mind that Timothy is, like Paul, a travelling missionary and church-planting evangelist. Never mind that Titus is also not a pastor but has been "left behind in Crete" to help establish a church community there before he moves on to plant other churches elsewhere. Never mind that Philemon isn't anything other than a slave owner who needs encouragement from Paul regarding treatment of said slave. Never mind that both of the epistles to Timothy and the one to Titus deal primarily with the character of elders (plural) within the church community. Never mind that the word "Pastor" does not appear in any of these so-called "Pastoral Epistles." Never mind that the word "Pastor" only appears once in the entire New Testament, and then it is in the plural.

As long as you can overlook all of these minor details, you should have no problem referring to these as the "Pastoral Epistles" of Paul.

WHAT DOES IT MEAN TO BE A MINISTER?

The definition of the world "minister" from the original Greek, according to Strong's Concordance:

"One who executes the commands of another, esp. of a master, a servant, attendant, minister." 1a) the servant of a king; 1b) a deacon, one who, by virtue of the office assigned to him by the church, cares for the poor and has charge of and distributes the money collected for their use; 1c) a waiter, one who serves food and drink.

It's fascinating that most think of a Minister as the power-tie wearing, spiritual authority figure and CEO of the local Christian franchise.

Wouldn't it be awesome if pastors and ministers simply loved and served people because it was what God called them to do and not because they were being paid handsomely?

As I've been exploring spiritual gifts and how God uses them in the Body, I've realized that all spiritual gifts are for the benefit of others, not ourselves. The gift to shepherd is intended to provide spiritual care for the rest of the Body, not a position of authority and power to be "Lorded over" the people of God.

If being a shepherd is a gift from God, like the spiritual gift of encouragement or administration or speaking in tongues, this means that a twelve-year-old girl could have the gift to pastor or shepherd others.

It also means that one could attend seminary and command a high salary at a mega-church and not have the gift to pastor at all.

> IF BEING A SHEPHERD IS A GIFT FROM GOD, LIKE THE SPIRITUAL GIFT OF ENCOURAGEMENT OR ADMINISTRATION OR SPEAKING IN TONGUES, THIS MEANS THAT A TWELVE-YEAR-OLD GIRL COULD HAVE THE GIFT TO PASTOR OR SHEPHERD OTHERS.

God gives this gift to His people in order to make sure they are cared for and loved and are spiritually healthy, not so that some can be the center of attention at the expense of others.

Most of us, when we think of the word "Pastor" get a mental image of a guy in a suit who stands up on the big stage each

Sunday and gives a long, power-pointed speech right after the offering plate is passed. But, that is not what Biblical pastoring is about at all.

Even though the New Testament is largely silent on the subject, our churches today have made the pastor the single most important position within the Body of Christ. As John H. Yoder points out:

> "There are few more reliable constants running through all human society than the special place every human community makes for the professional religionist…in every case he disposes a unique quality, which he usually possesses for life, which alone qualifies him for his function, and beside which the mass of men are identifiable negatively as "laymen," i.e., non-bearers of this special quality…One person per place is enough to do what he needs to do…the clergyman mediates between the common life and the realm of the "invisible" or the "spiritual"…No one balks at what his services cost."[2]

To be sure, God does provide people within the Body of Christ to help shepherd or pastor us. However, our mental pictures of this function are way off base. We picture a CEO in a power tie, but the Scriptures suggest a simple person who knows how to wash feet.

The word "Minister" implies one who serves, and yet in our society we've made the position into a professional office where all authority and power, prestige and wisdom flow down from on high.

Jesus modeled something so much greater for us when he put on the robes of a slave and knelt down to wash the feet of his disciples. He served them. The scriptures say that, He expressed the "fullness of his love" to them in this simple act of service and humility. What's more, when he was finished he sat down and asked them, *"Do you know what I have done for you?"* He wanted them to understand the importance of serving one another, not "Lording it over" their subjects as the Pharisees were known to do.

If we're honest, most of what passes for Pastoral leadership today looks a whole lot more like the "Lording it over" process modeled by the Pharisees than it does like the "putting on the robe of a servant" as Jesus did.

Honestly, the shepherd is simply one who has been gifted by the Holy Spirit to serve others. God is the One who calls people and then gives them the spiritual gift of a pastor. This means that you could go to seminary and get a degree, but still not have the genuine spiritual gift of a pastor, or shepherd, in God's family.

It also means you could be a teenager or a house wife and have a greater spiritual gift to lovingly shepherd your brothers and sisters in the Body than the guy who is standing behind the pulpit in the suit and tie with the seminary degree on the wall.

True shepherding means dying to yourself. It means giving up your time in order to meet with people who are in crisis. It means long hours in prayer for your dear brothers and sisters in Christ. It sometimes means helping them to repent, or to ask forgiveness. It means helping them make sense of their pain, or their loss. It means speaking truth to them even though they might hate you for it. It means standing aside and being silent in order to allow them to speak and to soar and to utilize the spiritual gifting that God has placed within them. It means rejoicing when they are honored in the assembly.

This is what it means to be a pastor in God's house. It means to serve, to minister to others, to shepherd people, and to love them so much that you're willing to do what's best for them, even if it kills you.

CAN WOMEN BE LEADERS IN THE CHURCH?

Some are convinced that there are New Testament scriptures which prohibit a woman to act as a leader within the Body. Before we take a look at those verses more closely I would like to remind everyone of the fact that women played a very important role in the ministry of Jesus.

His most powerful interactions, healings and teachings involve women (the woman at the well, the woman caught in adultery, the woman with the issue of blood, the woman whose son had died, the woman who anointed his feet with her tears and dried them with her hair, the woman who broke the box of perfume over his feet, etc.) and women supported his ministry, watched him die, attended his grave and gave witness to his resurrection from the dead.

Jesus honored women in a culture where women were undervalued and equal to children and unbelievers. Often they were treated more as property than as people.

WHAT PAUL SAYS

Now, let's see what Paul really had to say about this subject and, beyond that, what he meant to teach us about the role that women play in the Body.

In 1 Timothy 2:12 Paul says:

"I do not permit a woman to teach or to have authority over a man; she must be silent."

As with all difficult teachings and doctrine, we have to take the consensus of other scriptures on the subject in order to get a clear picture of what is actually being said and taught.

While Paul's statement here appears to be the final word on the matter, we have to remember that elsewhere Paul also teaches that a woman should cover her head when she prophesies. (1 Corinthians 11:4-5)

What's going on here? In one verse Paul says that he doesn't allow a woman to speak and he doesn't allow a woman to teach, yet in this passage he's providing guidelines for how a woman should prophesy in the gathering of believers.

Let me remind you that, to Paul, the gift of prophecy is one of the greatest "leadership" gifts in the entire Body (see 1 Corinthians 14: 1-5). Doesn't one who prophesies speak to the entire Body and provide a message from God for their edification and strengthening?

How do we reconcile these seemingly contradictory ideas regarding Paul's vision of Church? Women are allowed to prophesy as long as their heads are covered, and yet they are called to keep silent. What's going on?

In my opinion, there are a few things going on here. First, Paul says one thing to the Church in Corinth because he is addressing some very specific issues they are facing in their fellowship together. This means that when he writes to Timothy and he gives a different set of guidelines he is attempting to correct a different set of behaviors within a different Body of believers.

Simply put, the church where Timothy was serving didn't face the same problems as the church in Corinth. Therefore, Paul's advice to one was not the same as what was given to the other.

Also, Paul often says certain controversial things and he attaches a qualifier like, "I am saying this, and not the LORD..." as he does in 1 Corinthians 7:12, "But to the rest I, not the Lord, say, If any brother has a wife who does not believe, and she is willing to be with him, let him not divorce her."

In passages like this Paul seems to be aware of certain opinions that he might hold that may, or may not, be necessarily a hardline teaching from God.

With this in mind, I think it's interesting that in our original passage (1 Tim 2:11-12), Paul says, "I do not allow a woman to teach or to have authority over a man…" and in my mind this leaves room for us to wonder out loud about whether or not Paul intended this teaching to be taken as "from the Lord" or from Paul's personal bag of wisdom. Some scholars have pointed out that for Paul to add the qualifier, "I do not allow" he was admitting that other Apostles in the Church at this time did allow it.

Furthermore, other scholars have made note that the passage, in the Greek, actually is better translated as "I am not now allowing," which suggests that Paul may have been speaking to a special circumstance that needed to be addressed. At any rate, I believe Paul leaves room for us to disagree with him in these matters of cultural preference regarding the role of women within the gathering. I want to stress, however, that we do not have that same privilege when Paul leaves off that qualifier, "I, not the Lord."

WOMEN AS DEACONS, ELDERS AND LEADERS

Paul writes in Timothy and in Titus to provide criteria for an elder, and an overseer within the Body. In those passages he centers on the male gender, calling for them to be "Husbands of one wife," etc.

However, the New Testament also includes great evidence that the early church had many women deacons. Paul speaks of a deaconess named Phoebe in Romans 16:1 and also mentions Priscilla and Aquila in verse 2 calling them "my fellow workers in Christ Jesus." These two are also prominent in Paul's ministry, even traveling with him on Missionary journey's in Acts 18:18, and we know that the two of them hosted a church in their home according to 1 Corinthians 16:19. (Paul also mentions Euodia and Syntyche in Philipians 4, as well as Tabitha or Dorcas in Acts 9.)

Women are welcome to share among the rest of the people who gather to share and worship in the 1 Corinthians 12 model.

For more in-depth discussion of this important subject, please see my book, *Jesus Unbound: Liberating the Word of God from the Bible*. I also whole-heartedly recommend the book, *What's With Paul and Women?* by Jon Zens.

SPIRITUAL COVERING OR ACCOUNTABILITY?

Spiritual Covering is a concept built on fear and superstition, not on Biblical principles or values. Our house church believes in the Priesthood of the Believer. We believe that the Holy Spirit leads us into all Truth. We believe that the Word of God is active and powerful and effective to establish our Church and keep us on the path where Jesus walks.

Essentially, our house church is not under any official "Spiritual Covering" of any sort. We do, however, have loads and loads of spiritual accountability, which is Biblical. I have mentors who I can call on (and I often do) for advice, guidance, and insight. These are people like David Ruis, Todd Hunter, Jon Zens, and a few other men of God who are smarter and wiser than I am. At the same time, I am personally accountable to every person in our group. They are accountable to one another and also to me.

Our House Church is truly an independent endeavor. My wife and I left our previous church to start the house church without any official "covering" from any other church or organization.

To be honest, I never really felt a need to research the whole question of spiritual covering because God had called me to step out and launch our house church and there had been no hint that we needed to do this with the "blessing" or "covering" of any other leader or organized church. However, about a year into our journey one of our dear friends asked us about our spiritual covering. I wasn't sure how to respond. I had my own, very strong opinions about the subject already in place, but I decided to at least entertain the subject and ask some of the spiritual advisors in my life what their take on the subject might be.

So, I shot off an email to people like author Dallas Willard (author of "The Divine Conspiracy"), Todd Hunter (former National Director of Vineyard Churches), David Ruis (worship leader, author, songwriter), and also a few of my own personal mentors. These are made up of former pastors, chaplains, seminary graduates, and lay leaders. I asked them each to share with me their thoughts on the subject of "Spiritual Covering."

Quite honestly, I expected a robust series of heated debates on the concept. Of that list, only two of them had any real bias in favor of house churches. All the rest were either full-time pastors of traditional churches or at least former pastors. Their responses truly surprised me. They each agreed with my conviction that "Spiritual Covering" was simply not a Biblical concept as most people understand it.

First let me explain the basic idea behind "spiritual covering" here. Whenever someone, like myself for example, decides to start a church (house church or traditional), it is usually expected that the leader will submit his group to a higher organizational authority in order to protect the leader, and the new church, from doctrinal errors (heresy), and to protect against moral failures within the leadership staff.

This sounds like common sense, and I have to admit that if we were starting a traditional church, I might agree that such a system might be prudent. However, the House Church by design is already a highly accountable group of like-minded people. In the House Church model, it's hard to be anonymous for very long. There is a high level of accountability in our small group. Plus, I do not lecture as the resident Biblical expert in our house church. Everyone, no matter how young or how old, is free to share scripture and discuss the Bible at length. Because of this, it's much more difficult for heretical ideas to flourish very long. In fact, at times my own children have corrected me and pointed out my errors in dividing the Scriptures. This teaches me to be humble and it allows everyone else to test what is being said against the Scriptures.

In contrast, the traditional church makes it much easier for people to remain anonymous and to wear masks that suggest "everything is alright." A recent coffee meeting with a good friend of mine, who pastors a very large denominational church locally, confirmed this idea. He admitted that he usually hears about "secret sin" in His Body when the marriage is already over, or the surprise pregnancy has already taken place, etc. In our House Church, we encounter things on the front end, not the last gasp.

Each person who responded to my question about "Spiritual Covering" agreed that there was no Biblical foundation for such a teaching, although many churches use this as a way to control their leaders and manage their "flock" by fear.

Simply put, "Any church without spiritual covering is not, because of this fact, in error. However, if any church (with or without spiritual covering), believes or teaches or allows heretical ideas or doctrines or immoral activities to flourish, then that church is in error." I think one of the main things that came out of this larger discussion was the idea that spiritual accountability is Biblical, but spiritual covering is artificial, fear-based, man-made, and still not very effective in preventing doctrinal heresy or avoiding moral failures in the clergy.

Most of us who have been around for while in the Christian Church can testify that our best systems of accountability do not prevent adultery, heresy, embezzlement, etc. We've probably all seen good, godly men and women fall hard. Sometimes the ones who fall are the very last people we would ever expect to fail in such a way. Nevertheless, they do, and often.

As a former pastor, I have personally witnessed such failures over the last twenty years first-hand and it's never a pretty sight. Why do these things happen? Is it largely because we have elevated these leaders to an un-Biblical level? I would say, yes.

Spiritual covering is not the same as accountability. When I spoke to Todd Hunter about this he had a great quote that I thought really expressed how arbitrary this idea of covering is. He said that if Rick Warren or Chuck Smith (or some other Christian with a celebrity status or a successful ministry, book, or radio show) were to announce today that they were leaving to start a brand-new house church, no one would dare ask them, "Who is your spiritual covering?" But if you or I (or some other "regular guy") were to hear God's call to start simple house church, then suddenly the question of "Spiritual Covering" arises. Suddenly it's just too dangerous to do this without another, higher spiritual authority looking out for things.

The truth is, when Chuck Smith left the Foursquare denomination to start Calvary Chapel, he had no spiritual covering. When John Wimber left Calvary Chapel to launch the Vineyard Movement, he also had no spiritual covering. Does this mean that, to this very day, these large, international church-planting movements are without a spiritual covering? Yes, it does. Is that a problem? Not if you attend Calvary Chapel or a Vineyard church, and not if you reject the idea of "Covering" anyway.

For that matter, when Martin Luther left the Catholic Church of his day and started a Protestant Reformation, he also had no "Spiritual Covering" either. So, I suppose there is no need to go much further than this. For me, it boils down to whether or not you are convinced that there is such a thing as "The Priesthood of The Believer" and how you define it. Scripturally, I believe, that every follower of Jesus is qualified to use their God-given spiritual gifts without the approval of a denominational leader or an organization. Basically, there is no need for a spiritual "go-between." We might need accountability, or discipling, or encouragement, or sometimes even rebuke from one another, but it is not necessary that we have a man, or an organization, to stand between us and God.

A few years ago, some friends of mine wanted to start a Bible Study in their apartment. Because the lead pastor of the Church they were attending couldn't be there to oversee the study, they were not allowed to have their Bible Study. That is a prime example of the complete denial of the Priesthood of the Believer because "regular Christians" were not allowed to read the Bible on their own and understand it without the direct oversight of an official Church representative.

We might as well trade in our modern English Bibles for Latin ones and apologize for the Reformation if that is how we feel about things.

I realize that there are good people, sincere followers of Jesus who would disagree with me on this issue. I am not trying to argue or sling mud at anyone. However, it is my very strong opinion (and also, surprisingly, that of those distinguished gentlemen I surveyed earlier—smarter men than I, let us admit), that all that is needed for a Church to operate properly is to submit to one another, and to Christ, and to let the Scriptures (the Bible) be your guide. The Holy Spirit promised (and I really do believe Him) to lead us into all Truth. We do not need an expert or a professional to tell us we are "safe" or "official."

We are The Body of Christ. We are The Church. The Bible is our Statement of Faith. We are accountable to one another and to The Holy Spirit of God. Jesus if our Head and He will build His Church just as He pleases (1 Cor 12).

"A good man will remain faithful, even with a poor structure of accountability, and a degenerate man will frustrate and resist even the most iron-clad system of accountability," my friend Todd Hunter said to me. I must agree.

> "A GOOD MAN WILL REMAIN FAITHFUL, EVEN WITH A POOR STRUCTURE OF ACCOUNTABILITY, AND A DEGENERATE MAN WILL FRUSTRATE AND RESIST EVEN THE MOST IRON-CLAD SYSTEM OF ACCOUNTABILITY."

I am happy to report that our House Church has accountability by the truck-load. I am accountable to every single person in our house church family. I am accountable to several other godly men with whom I am in constant relationship. I am also accountable to my wife and to my two sons.

Even so, I have seen enough pastors fall into sin and self-deception and pride to know that no one is immune from moral or doctrinal failure. Accountability is essential. We must submit ourselves to God, and to our brothers and sisters in Christ, or we will never avoid the sin which so easily entangles.

CHAPTER 3

REMEMBER THIS

A PROFOUND MYSTERY

When you consider that the Bible as we know it today was written over a period of thousands of years, by a wide variety of authors, and assembled as a single document nearly two thousand years ago, it's fairly miraculous that the first three chapters of the Bible correspond so symmetrically with the last three chapters of the Bible.

In the first three chapters of the Bible, in the book of Genesis, we see a series of events that are mirrored in the last three chapters of Revelation.

First, we see the creation of heaven and earth. At the end of Revelation we see a new creation.

In the first three chapters we see Satan ensnaring mankind and in the last three we see Satan cast down and doomed forever.

In the first three chapters we see a garden, and in the last three chapters we see a garden city. Both gardens include the tree of life.

In the first three chapters we have a curse given to man for his sins, and in the last three chapters the curse is forever removed.

In the first three chapters God visits the garden in the cool of the day, and in the last three chapters God is at home with man forever.

In the first three chapters man and woman are cast out, but in the last three chapters they are welcomed in.

In the first three chapters a bride is created from out of Adam's side, and in the last three chapters a Bride is ushered in for the Son of God and a wedding feast is celebrated.

In the first three chapters we have the beginning of Time, and in the last three we have the beginning of Eternity.

DEEPER THINGS

The Scriptures reveal the Church to be the Bride of the Lamb. It is one of the most common metaphors used by God to describe His people throughout the Bible. However, if we begin to trace these threads between Genesis and Revelation we will notice even more about what Paul the Apostle refers to as "a profound mystery."

In Ephesians, Paul uses the metaphor of marriage to teach us something astounding about Jesus and about our identity as the Bride of Christ. I've edited the text to highlight the main thoughts:

> "...just as Christ loved the church and gave himself up for her to make her holy, cleansing her by the washing with water through the word, and to present her to himself as a radiant church, without stain or wrinkle or any other blemish, but holy and blameless." (Eph 5:25-27)

> "'For this reason a man will leave his father and mother and be united to his wife, and the two will become one flesh.' This is a profound mystery — but I am talking about Christ and the church." (Eph 5:31-32)

Because this passage is so often used to counsel men and women in regards to the marriage relationship, I have removed those references so that we can see what Paul says he is actually talking about: "Christ and the church."

First, Paul tells us how Christ has given himself up for us (the Bride) and how he cleanses and washes us through the word of God so that we might be ready for our wedding day. Paul also quotes from Genesis chapter 2 in this passage and this reminds us of how God put Adam to sleep and made a woman for him because "God saw that it was not good for man to be alone."

Notice it was God's idea, not Adam's, for man to have a wife. Somehow this reference points to God's plan for the Church. As Paul reminds us, "For this reason" the man is to "leave his father and mother and be united with his wife and the two will become one flesh." This is where Paul pauses and remarks that "this is a profound mystery." Why? Because he is not talking about Adam and Eve now. He's not talking about Christian marriage between a man and a woman. No, he is talking about Jesus and the Church "becoming one flesh."

THE MYSTERY OF THE BRIDE

We know from Scripture that we (the Church) are the Bride of Christ (Eph 5:22-33). But in Revelation we learn that the Bride is also a City:

> "One of the seven angels who had the seven bowls full of the seven last plagues came and said to me, 'Come, I will show you the bride, the wife of the Lamb.' And he carried me away in the Spirit to a mountain great and high, and showed me the Holy City, Jerusalem, coming down out of heaven from God." (Rev 21:9-10)

We are the Bride, and the Bride is a City.

THE MYSTERY OF THE TEMPLE

We also know that we are the Temple of God (Eph 2:21), but in Revelation we discover that it is Christ who is the Temple in us:

> "The great street of the city was of pure gold, like transparent glass. I did not see a temple in the city, because the Lord God Almighty and the Lamb are its temple." (Rev 21:21-22)

So, we are the Temple where God dwells within, but we are also the Bride which is a city and in that city is a Temple which is the Lord Himself.

ONE IN CHRIST JESUS

Want to see how this is played out in the rest of the Scriptures? In the Gospel of John, beyond the prayer of Jesus to the Father that we (the Bride) would be one even as Jesus and the Father are one, Christ also prays:

> "Father, just as you are in me and I am in you. May they also be in us so that the world may believe that you have sent me. I have given them the glory that you gave me, that they may be one as we are one: I in them and you in me. May they be brought to complete unity to let the world know that you sent me and have loved them even as you have loved me." (John 17:21-23)

In Ephesians 2:21 we are told that we are the Temple of God, as we have already seen, but look at what this passage actually communicates. Try to guess where God ends and we begin here:

> "In him the whole building is joined together and rises to become a holy temple in the Lord. And in him you too are being built together to become a dwelling in which God lives by his Spirit." (Eph 2:21-22)

Here we see that we (the Church, the Bride, the Body and the Temple) are being built to become a dwelling in which God lives, and yet the Temple is being built "in him." So, we are being built in Christ to become a Temple where God will dwell by His Spirit. Who is on the inside? Who is dwelling where? We are in Christ, and we contain God's Spirit all at the same time.

THE MYSTERY OF THE BODY

In 1 Corinthians 12, and in Ephesians 4:15, Paul gives us another wonderful illustration of how the Body is to function. He refers to the Church as the Body of Christ and explains that we are dependent upon one another for life, and yet that Christ is our Head and without Him we can do nothing (see also John 15:5). Here we have a wonderful picture of the unity which Jesus prayed we would have (John 17:21-23) and a fulfillment of the picture that we are "one flesh" (Genesis 2:24, Eph 2:21), with Christ since we are His Body and He is our head.

As I look at who we are in Christ, (His Body, Temple and Bride), and as I see God's sovereign plan from the beginning (to find a Bride for His Son, and a Temple for His presence), and as I hear the prayer of Jesus that we be in Him and that we be one even as He and the Father are one, I cannot help but feel an urgency to tear down our man-made divisions and embrace our identity as members of one Body, with one Head.

THE GLORIOUS MYSTERY OF GOD

This mystery is quite profound. One worthy of our awe. It is not my goal to explain or understand this mystery. One dear brother I shared this with recently said to me, "Let it continue to be a mystery in your heart" and that is my intention. This is a profound mystery and what we must contemplate is not how to make sense of it, but instead how to live out our part of it.

How can we be one in Christ? How can we make Christ the head of our Church? How can we be the Temple of the Living God? How can we make ourselves ready for that glorious wedding day to come?

THE END IS THE BEGINNING

The last thing I see as I look at the symmetry between Genesis and Revelation is that all of History ends with a wedding. All that we have known, and all that we now experience is only the courtship. This is just the engagement phase of our life with Christ. One day we will become the Bride of Christ and be one with Him. Yet, a wedding is not the end of life, it is only the beginning.

Scripture ends with a beginning. This is a very profound mystery, indeed.

WE ARE THE CHURCH

A good friend of mine once blurted out, "I hate church." It took me by surprise at first, but I can totally understand what my friend meant by that statement. He means that he hates the way people operate in the church, and that he's frustrated by the mentality of some people who are confused about what church is meant to be on this earth.

Honestly, whenever I see pastors manipulating their flocks, or when I see Christians spending the bulk of the offering on themselves, or when I see people twist the ideas of service, worship and faith, I also feel anger. I confess that there have been times when I have also been tempted to say, "I hate church."

But, I've been very encouraged to consider the words of A. W. Tozer on this subject when he reminds us that we are not speaking of some anonymous organization "out there" whenever we speak of "the Church." Instead, we are speaking about a living organism we are inextricably connected to for eternity.

We are the Church. So, while we may hate certain aspects of how our brothers and sisters operate, or how people act within the Body, we are still speaking of something that we are part of.

WE ARE THE CHURCH. THE ONLY CHURCH THE WORLD WILL EVER KNOW. THE ONLY CHURCH THERE WILL EVER BE.

We are the Church. The only Church the world will ever know. The only Church there will ever be.

So, now, let's go and be the church we dream of. If we want the Church to be more loving we must become more loving. If we want the Church to be more understanding and patient, we must become more understanding and patient.

As we've already seen from 1 Peter chapter 2, as we come to Jesus we are built up to become the people, and the Church, He is building.

Notice, God is the one doing the building. He is accomplishing all of this as He builds us up into the people He wants us to be—A holy priesthood which embodies the Spirit of God as a living temple.

I know it can seem very simplistic to consider this, but all we have to do is to come to Jesus and allow Him (by the power of His Holy Spirit) to build us up into the people He has called and designed and intended for us to be.

In our churches today we have relied too heavily on ourselves, our own leaders, and our own ideas of doing church. I believe that every Christian, whether denominational or independent, charismatic or conservative, must ask themselves this question: "Are we truly relying on God for our health and existence or are we relying on other people or things?"

As my friend Alan Knox points out:

"If removing leadership or programs or buildings or finances or anything else would cause believers to stop meeting together, stop disciplining one another, stop growing spiritually, then that group of believers is not depending on God.

For those of us who are leaders, this is an especially important question. If the church would stop functioning or growing if we disappeared, then there's a big problem. We are…building something that depends on us, not on the Holy Spirit.

We may birth something on our own, and we may keep something running on our own. But, only the Spirit can birth and grow a church."[1]

CHURCH = GOD + THE PEOPLE OF GOD

We've gotten into the bad habit of thinking that Church equals a paid professional clergyman, and a building that must be paid for and maintained, and a strategy to attract people to fill the seats, etc. But none of that is in the New Testament. It's not how Jesus modeled Church for us. It's not how the Disciples and the Apostles went about planting and growing Churches for nearly 400 years.

We have to stop trying to build the Church and start being the Church. Let Him build His Church. Let's start learning to be the Church, and the people, He has called us to be.

IN PROCESS

One thing that I've learned over the last few years is that all of us are in process. Opinions I held a few years ago have been replaced by new convictions, and things I would never have dreamed of before are now more real to me than I could have ever imagined.

Because of this I am learning how to have grace for others who may not agree with me about certain things. I often ask for them to extend grace to me as well.

Following Jesus has been an adventure for me. This roller coaster ride is really only beginning, I know. So, there's really no easy way to end this book. Every week I learn something new and I discover something amazing that I have to share with our house church family or with those who follow my blog.

I hope this book has been a blessing to you, and I hope that at least some of what I have shared about God's desire for a Church that embodies His Spirit and lives out His love for others has been encouraging to you.

If you have any questions or insights regarding what you've read here, I would love to hear from you.

May God continue to challenge you as you seek His face and may you always have the courage to walk with Him wherever He calls you to go.

CHAPTER 4

ANATOMY OF AN OPEN MEETING

WHAT IS AN OPEN MEETING?

An open meeting is one where everyone in the gathering is as free as anyone else to speak, or to share, or to teach, or to sing, etc., as the Holy Spirit leads them.

This sort of meeting is what Paul was describing in 1 Corinthians 12 where he begins by explaining how various spiritual gifts are distributed throughout the church and then uses a Body metaphor to describe how these gifts are designed to function in a practical way.

> "There are different kinds of gifts, but the same Spirit distributes them. There are different kinds of service, but the same Lord. There are different kinds of working, *but in all of them and in everyone* it is the same God at work." (1 Cor. 12:4-6; emphasis mine)

Right off the bat, Paul explains that there are different kinds of gifts, and also that the purpose of them is to work "in all of them" (the members of the church) and he emphasizes that "everyone" is expected to participate. Not only a select few. As he goes on to say in the next verse:

"Now *to each one* the manifestation of the Spirit *is given for the common good.*" (1 Cor. 12:7)

Here, he re-emphasizes that "each one" is given the spiritual gift "for the common good" of everyone else in the church gathering.

NOTICE THAT PAUL DOESN'T SAY THAT THE MANIFESTATIONS OF THE SPIRIT ARE GIVEN FOR A SELECT FEW, OR TO ONE MAN, BUT TO "EVERYONE" AND THAT "EACH ONE" RECEIVES A DIFFERENT GIFT IN ORDER TO BE A GIFT TO EVERYONE ELSE.

This tells us that the spiritual gifts are not to edify or build up the person using the gift, but to lovingly bless and minister to everyone else in the church fellowship. Therefore, the spiritual gifts are "in all of them" and "everyone" is gifted to be a blessing "for the common good" of their brothers and sisters.

Notice that Paul doesn't say that the manifestations of the Spirit are given for a select few, or to one man, but to "everyone" and that "each one" receives a different gift in order to be a gift to everyone else. This is the groundwork for an open meeting of Christians.

After listing a series of spiritual gifts that might be given to the members ("Message of wisdom", "faith", "gifts of healing", etc.), Paul again says:

"All these are the work of one and the same Spirit, and *he distributes them to each one*, just as he determines." (1 Cor. 12:11)

Just in case we've forgotten, Paul reminds us that "each one" receives a gift from God in the church in order to facilitate the work of the Spirit in the church when they gather.

Next, Paul goes on to explain that the Body (which is a metaphor for how the Church should function), is one, even though it is made up of many parts. He then takes time to illustrate how the church is designed on purpose to be a group of very different sorts of people. Not a homogenous cookie-cutter group of clones, but a gathering of people who are not like one another. He talks about how those who are "feet" cannot say they are not part of this body because they are not like the "hands", and he goes on to stress that the "eyes" cannot kick out the "hands" because they are different. Therefore, differences are to be expected—even celebrated—and this is because the variety is part of what makes us a body of many parts. He closes the chapter by saying:

> "But God has put the body together, giving greater honor to the parts that lacked it, so that *there should be no division in the body*, but *that its parts should have equal concern for each other. If one part suffers, every part suffers with it*; if one part is honored, every part rejoices with it.

> "Now you are the body of Christ, and *each one of you is a part of it.*" (1 Cor. 12:24-27)

This is really only the ground work for what an open meeting of believers should look like. Paul explains how the gifts of the Spirit are distributed to everyone in the Church using the metaphor of a Body that is made up of different parts that serve different functions, and he makes the point that these parts are all essential for the life of the Body.

This means that if you are a follower of Christ, you have a spiritual gift from God. It means you have a very crucial role to play in the growth and development of the Church family where you are a member. It means that you matter. You are important. We need you, and you need all of us.

What I find fascinating is that Paul follows this chapter about how a gathering of believers can operate like a Body with an entire chapter on love. He does this twice more in Ephesians 4 and in Romans 12. Every time Paul talks about spiritual gifts in the Body, the very next thing he talks about is love. Why? Because the gifts are given in love, and they only work if we use

BECAUSE THE GIFTS ARE GIVEN IN LOVE, AND THEY ONLY WORK IF WE USE THEM OUT OF LOVE TO BLESS THE BROTHERS AND SISTERS WE LOVE IN ORDER TO HELP THEM TO GROW INTO THE IMAGE OF CHRIST WHO IS LOVE.

them out of love to bless the brothers and sisters we love in order to help them to grow into the image of Christ who is love.

Later, in 1 Corinthians 14, Paul returns to this idea of how everyone in the Body is expected to operate together for the common good, saying:

"What then shall we say, brothers and sisters? *When you come together, each of you* has a hymn, or a word of instruction, a revelation, a tongue or an interpretation. *Everything must be done so that the church may be built up.*" (1 Cor. 14:26)

Again, Paul returns to the theme he laid out in chapter 12. The command is, "When you come together, each of you" uses their God-given gifts for the common good. Why? Because, as Paul goes on to say, this kind of symbiotic sharing of love and ministry is essential and "must be done so that the church may be built up."

This isn't an optional method for gathering that Paul outlines for us here. Paul is emphatic that "each one" of us should use our gifts "for the common good" and that it "must be done" for the "church" to be "built up."

You can quickly see how a Pastor-centric church will never operate in this way as Paul describes. Because with a professional expert in the room, everyone will always turn to that person and wait for instructions. But, Paul doesn't make any room for this aberration. Nor does anyone else in the New Testament scriptures.

An open meeting embraces Paul's instructions here and in other passages to operate as a true body where Christ is the head

(Eph. 4:15)—the only head—and we all "submit to one another out of reverence for Christ." (Eph. 5:21)

WHAT DOES AN OPEN MEETING LOOK LIKE?

Essentially, what we try to do is to come together and "take hold of Christ" as a Body. In other words, try to imagine that your church was sitting together in someone's living room and suddenly Jesus walks in the door and stands in the center of the room.

Would you guys keep talking to one another about the weather, or sports, or even Bible verses? Hopefully you'd all sit quietly and lean forward to hear what Jesus wanted to say to you. You'd talk to Him, not to each other. You'd meet with Him, not have a meeting about Him while He watched. That's basically what we're trying to do every time we meet.

Now, it might look different each time. And sometimes, honestly, we're better at it than at other times. But, usually our times together go something like this:

Some of us meet about thirty minutes early for prayer before the meeting starts. A brother once noted that an open meeting requires more prayer together, not less. This is because an open meeting is led by the Spirit, not by any one person or persons. Everyone is invited to this prayer time, but no one has to come if they don't want to.

After prayer everyone else shows up for a shared, potluck breakfast together. Eating is an essential ingredient, I believe. It helps us to get to know one another and to be together without being pretentious. It's also how we build community and find out what people are like, what they're going through, etc. Real ministry can take place during the meal times, or we can just laugh together and eat some great food. Either way it's worth the

investment of time. Plus, it's based on the practice of the earliest
Christians:

> "They devoted themselves to the apostles' teaching and to fel-
> lowship, to the breaking of bread and to prayer." (Acts 2:42)

> "They broke bread in their homes and ate together with glad
> and sincere hearts…" (Acts 2:46)

Eventually we'll finish eating and gather around the sofas and
set out the communion elements and wait quietly for a while to
pray together before we start singing songs. The singing is always
suggested by the members of the Body, or anyone in the room.
We have a set of worship songs put together in a songbook format, and we also have a set of old Baptist Hymnals. Or someone
can bring a CD with a song to share, or they can just start singing a song that they love a cappella and either teach it to all of
us, or let those who know it join in.

There's lots of flexibility, as you'll notice. We're very conscious
of the fact that we're not putting on a show. We're not trying to
shush the children or keep to a program. We just try to allow the
Holy Spirit to move however He likes and get out of His way.

During the singing time someone might feel led to read a
scripture out loud, or to pray for someone else in the group, or
to call out to God in thanksgiving and praise. We never know
how that might work, but we're open to whatever happens.

I think this can only work if you're with a group of people,
a family of believers, that you can trust. You have to know that
everyone in that meeting cares for you and loves you. They're
not trying to control you or to manipulate you. Over the last six
years we've been developing that level of trust together and it's
great, really.

Eventually we'll move from the singing and prayer time to
"open share time" where everyone (young, old, male, female,

visitor, regular, etc.) is free to share with everyone else what God has been teaching them during the week, or to share something that the Lord spoke to them during worship, etc. But not everyone has to share. It's ok to be quiet and listen, too.

Transition from the singing to the open share time is very fluid and sometimes we'll drift back into singing songs again, or spend the whole time praying for one another, or maybe share with one another over a single passage of scripture, or a variety of scriptures if there are a lot of people who have something to share. It varies week to week.

WHAT I REALLY LOVE IS WHEN THE SEEMINGLY RANDOM VERSES AND TESTIMONIES THAT EACH PERSON BRINGS SUDDENLY BEGIN TO EMERGE AS A COMPLETE TEACHING ON A SINGLE TOPIC.

What I really love is when the seemingly random verses and testimonies that each person brings suddenly begin to emerge as a complete teaching on a single topic. Sometimes someone will say, "What is Jesus trying to teach us this morning?" and we'll realize "Oh, it's about letting go and trusting Him" or "It's about forgiveness", and then we'll try to respond to Him and thank Him for teaching us this lesson as a Body.

Our meetings usually run from about 9am for morning prayer to around 1pm or so. Sometimes it goes to 2pm but usually 12:30pm to 1pm. We usually end with Communion together and sing a song before we depart.

Now, even though this is our usual meeting format, what I love about an organic church is that we always have freedom to change things around whenever the Lord directs us to.

In the past, we've had gatherings where everyone creates artwork together, or perhaps we hear a testimony from someone, or sometimes we'll hear a teaching by someone who brings a study on a particular topic or book of the Bible. Sometimes we'll meet in a park together, or spend all of our time in worship and prayer.

Breaking our liturgy and embracing our freedom in Christ to do something different is important to the life of the Body.

One of my favorite times was when we asked the children to lead our meeting. They all sat together and we waited to see what they would do. Then one of them said, "Ok, does anyone have something to share with the group today?"

It was so wonderful because they had learned from us that to lead a meeting is to ask questions and invite others to share. How cool is that?

HOW DO I LEAD AN OPEN MEETING?

This is probably the hardest thing to write about. As someone who grew up in the traditional church, was trained to be a leader in the church and has never even attended an open meeting before transitioning to an open house church model, leading others in this kind of meeting is very difficult to do.

For the first several years of our house church gatherings, I tried to encourage this sort of open meeting. Sometimes we would manage to come close, but it was years really before we started to actually have the sort of open meetings we long for.

If anything, the leader in an open meeting should begin by exercising great self-control and restraint. Honestly, a successful open meeting is more about what I *don't do* than anything I do to make it successful. For example, I don't prepare a teaching every time we gather. I don't answer every question about the Bible that comes up.

> "BE THE BIBLE QUESTION MAN, NOT THE BIBLE ANSWER MAN"

(As Neil Cole suggest, "Be the Bible Question Man, not the Bible Answer Man"). I don't decide in advance what we'll talk about or what we'll study. I don't choose the worship songs ahead of time. I don't orchestrate the meeting. I don't fill the awkward silences with noise. I don't create a dependency on myself. I don't lead the communion time. I don't have a follow-up or illustration to wrap up everyone else's testimony or scripture verse.

So, once we know what we don't want to do, what is it that we *should* be doing? For starters, we should spend time in prayer before the meeting to ask the Lord Jesus to reveal Himself and have His way in the gathering. We should allow everyone a chance to speak. We should make sure the quietest person in the room is invited to share something, if they would like to. We should respect the opinions of others, even if they are not our own. We should learn how to disagree agreeably, which is all about your focus. If your focus is on Jesus then you won't get distracted so easily by disagreements on doctrine.

We should try to keep the group focused on Jesus if things begin to stray off the mark. We should learn to ask intelligent and insightful questions more than we bring clever answers to show our intelligence. We should find ways to bless everyone else in the group. We should pray during the meeting for the Lord to speak, and to move, and to have His way, and to reveal His heart to everyone. We should listen to the Holy Spirit if He prompts us to stop and pray for someone in need, or to sit quietly and listen for His voice, or to sing another song to respond to something inspiring we've just heard someone share with us. We should allow others to lead the group as they hear from the Lord. We should not see ourselves as leaders filling a position of authority but as servants fulfilling Christ's command to serve others in love.

Overall, the leaders of an open meeting should be seen and almost never heard unless it's necessary.

OVERALL, THE LEADERS OF AN OPEN MEETING SHOULD BE SEEN AND ALMOST NEVER HEARD UNLESS IT'S NECESSARY.

Granted, there are times when a visitor, or even a regular member, might become hostile, or attempt to take over the group or monopolize the share time. That's when the leaders in the Body need to defend everyone else in the group and lovingly suggest that there might be someone else who would like to share something. If that doesn't work, you might need to pull this person aside after the meeting and explain to them how an open meeting is designed to work and why it's better if they take time to listen more than they share so that others can participate and everyone can grow together.

THE DANGER OF CREATING HEROES AND EXPERTS

I've shared my concerns about elevating leaders within the House Church/Organic Church movement to become our own versions of "Pastors" and "Bishops." If we do that we've now become as guilty as the rest of the traditional church we left behind in order to pursue Christ as our only Head.

This is a two way street, by the way. It can be the Leader who seeks the fame and the name, or it can be the people who seek after a guru who will tell them what to believe and how to behave. Or, it can be a little of both.

As someone whose personal sin is Pride, I have to admit that I'm very aware of this tendency in myself and I work very hard to sit in the background of our own church family and not take the Lord's place in the Body. I used to limit myself to only two "soap box moments" every meeting. Then my goal was to try not to share a comment on what every person shared during the meeting (which created a sort of conversational ping-pong where someone would share and then I would comment and then another person would share and then I would comment again, etc.). Now my goal is to keep silent unless the

Lord really prompts me to share something. Otherwise, I sit quietly and I listen.

I know that sometimes people who read my blog or my books will visit our house church and they'll expect that I'll have some cool teaching to share every time. But that's not what happens. If anything, I'll rarely talk at all unless the Lord has given me something to teach or to share.

I'll never forget when one brother visited our group for the first time after reading my blog. He came on a Thursday evening and after I played the guitar during the shared worship time, I got up and left the room. He told me later that he thought it was very weird that I would do that, but the group didn't miss a beat and people were sharing and teaching and praying for one another spontaneously without me in the room. Eventually he did notice that I had returned to the room when I spoke up and shared something, but until that moment he was oblivious to my presence, which is sort of the point, really.

My goal is really to encourage everyone else to share. I really want to hear what my two teenage boys have to say. I want to hear from those quiet wives who never speak out. I want to hear what that five year old boy has to say about Jesus. Those are always the most profound things, really. I've learned so much from the most unlikely sources. It's amazing, really.

MY GOAL IS REALLY TO ENCOURAGE EVERYONE ELSE TO SHARE...THOSE ARE ALWAYS THE MOST PROFOUND THINGS, REALLY. I'VE LEARNED SO MUCH FROM THE MOST UNLIKELY SOURCES. IT'S AMAZING, REALLY.

This kind of thing is a movement of God. No man can take credit for this. When I hear from people all over the nation, and even the world, that God is leading them in this same New Testament model of "being Church" it excites me. Because we're not moving in this direction because we read a blog or a book or attended a conference. Every one I've spoken to shares their story about how God did this to them. God called them to step outside the traditional model of Church and they obeyed Him and followed His leading, even at a great cost—usually friendships, or salaries, or the respect of others, etc. But when I hear those testimonies I rejoice because I know that God is purifying His Bride and He's doing something marvelous that no man can dare take credit for.

WHAT DO LEADERS ACTUALLY DO?

Let's take some time to talk about things that leaders (or "elders") in the open meeting or new testament church should be prepared to do, as-needed.

MAKING DISCIPLES

The purpose of the Church is to disciple others to follow Christ and to obey everything that He commands. Obedience to Christ, then, is critical to the life of the Body, and our gatherings together should be one of the primary places we learn how to follow Christ together on a daily basis.

Discipleship, I believe, is not always a leader/student arrangement where the mature Christian is teaching the baby Christian how to follow Christ. Not that it can't be that way, of course, but I don't believe it's the only way we make disciples.

In our house church family I've found that a by-product of our fellowship together is a sort of constant discipleship where the Body works together to help everyone else follow Christ daily. It's an ongoing reality where we are learning together how to follow Christ personally.

The reality is, everyone is a disciple who helps to make disciples within the Body of Christ, and everyone is being discipled by everyone else.

This isn't a leader-to-student model. This is a brother-to-brother and sister-to-sister model. And a sister-to-brother-to-sister-to brother model.

Everyone gets to be a disciple and everyone gets to be discipled.

DEALING WITH CONFLICT

As an elder in the Body of Christ, one of our roles is to deal with conflict when it arises. It might be an argument between individuals in the group, or it might a divisive person who stirs things up, or it might be a disagreement over an issue of doctrine or a point of contention over a practice in the Body.

Our group has had a variety of these issues over the last six years. Sometimes the issues are trivial, and other times they are challenging. As always, spend time on your knees asking the Lord how to proceed. Remember, Jesus is the one who is building His church, not you or I. Always, continually, submit everything to Jesus and allow Him to move and to lead your church family through this process of healing and reconciliation.

DISCIPLINE

Sometimes, a leader might have to confront a member who needs to be disciplined, and for that I recommend a group of elders within the Body who are motivated by love and full of wisdom and Godly insight. The goal is always reconciliation and restoration. Be as discreet and private as possible as long as the person is cooperative and repentant. Only take things to the entire church body as a very last resort, and then again, only with the desire to bring repentance, reconciliation and restoration.

GUARDING YOUR FAMILY

Sometimes there are predators who come into your church family and you need to have discernment to recognize them and move quickly to remove them. This might involve meeting with them in person to let them know why you're asking them to leave, or you might need to pull them aside and give them a warning if you think they just need a friendly reminder to change their behaviors.

The kinds of behaviors we need to be wary of are those who cause division or strife in the Body:

> "I urge you, brothers and sisters, to watch out for those who cause divisions and put obstacles in your way that are contrary to the teaching you have learned. Keep away from them." (Romans 16:17)

Also look out for those who seek to have their way or to run the show. If this is something that you're not called to do, then it's certainly not something that anyone else has the right to do:

> "I wrote to the church, but Diotrephes, *who loves to be first*, will not welcome us. So when I come, I will call attention to what he is doing, spreading malicious nonsense about us. Not satisfied with that, he even refuses to welcome other believers. He also stops those who want to do so and puts them out of the church." (3 John 1:8-10)

Rather than allow one person to have their way and drive others out of the church, you should step in with other elders and ask this person to leave if they cannot fellowship without throwing their weight around.

You, of course, need to watch out for people who claim to be Christians but who are actually not following Jesus at all. As Paul explains:

> "But now I am writing to you that *you must not associate with anyone who claims to be a brother or sister* but is sexually immoral or greedy, an idolater or slanderer, a drunkard or swindler. Do not even eat with such people." (1 Cor. 5:11)

What Paul means, literally, is that we should not allow these people to gather with us when we eat and fellowship as a Church.

As always, the goal is reconciliation and restoration in the Body, not to damage people or to condemn people. So, if you're doing this right, no one else in the Body will ever know that you've met with anyone to discuss anything because you're honoring the people you love, not engaging in gossip or slander.

SO, IF YOU'RE DOING THIS RIGHT, NO ONE ELSE IN THE BODY WILL EVER KNOW THAT YOU'VE MET WITH ANYONE TO DISCUSS ANYTHING BECAUSE YOU'RE HONORING THE PEOPLE YOU LOVE, NOT ENGAGING IN GOSSIP OR SLANDER.

Again, this is not about control. We don't want our church fellowships to be about making people act like us or think like us. Please don't use this as a license to police the behaviors of your church family.

DEFEND THE LIBERTY OF EVERYONE

This one, to me, is the most difficult but one of the most important things to remember in an open meeting. In our church family we like to say that "everyone is in process" and this means that we're all coming from different denominational backgrounds and we're all at different levels of maturity in various areas of our walk with Christ.

This means that we do not ever attempt to get everyone else in the Body to agree with us on every point of doctrine. Our group does not have any Statement of Faith for this very reason. Our only criteria for gathering together, and for accepting people into this Body is simply this: "Do you love Jesus? Are you actually seeking to follow Him in your daily life?" And if your answer is "Yes" then you are welcome to be a member of this Body.

All we ask is that you don't attempt to change us to believe what you believe and we promise not to try to change you to believe what we believe.

This simple attitude of liberty has allowed our group of former Baptists, Pentecostals, Charismatics, Methodists, Presbyterians, etc. to fellowship together for over six years without heated arguments over doctrine. We gather only to seek Jesus together and to help everyone else in the group to follow Him in their daily lives.

Unless you want to create a church that is full of people who act and think and believe just exactly the way you do (and to me that's a nightmare), I encourage you to learn how to disagree agreeably and to major on Christ when you come together, not on this or that little pet doctrine or theory.

You'll not only learn things from people who think different from you, you'll also fulfill Christ's desire that everyone in His Body be one, even as He and the Father are one. Our unity isn't based on agreement on doctrines, but on our sincere love for Christ alone.

CHAPTER 5

THE PITFALLS OF ORGANIC CHURCH

BREAK YOUR LITURGY

Early on in our house church experience we took the opportunity to embrace the boundless freedom of being the church together with our friends. Sometimes we would just eat together and share testimonies, other times we would plan to sit together outside on our patio and create a giant work of art on a shower curtain to express our passion for Jesus.

However, over time, we slowly settled into a more familiar groove that has now become our liturgy. We meet for a meal. We talk and eat. We eventually gather around and sing worship songs together. Then we have our open share time. We discuss the scriptures together. We pray for one another. We share communion. We dismiss. This is our liturgy.

My suggestion is that you do all that you can to upset the apple cart as often as possible in order to remind yourselves that you are free in Christ Jesus. You can meet anywhere—under a tree in the park, in a coffee shop, around the swimming pool, at the beach. You can do anything together—pray for an hour, sing spontaneously, create artwork, let the children lead the meeting, sit quietly and listen to the Holy Spirit, play games together, take turns sharing your testimony, invite an outside teacher to lead you through a book of the Bible, or wash one another's feet.

Whatever you do, the point is to escape the rut and to embrace the spontaneity of being church together. God always does something amazing whenever we put ourselves in a position where none of us really knows exactly what might happen next. That's where we're outside our comfort zones and the unexpected moment can catch us by surprise.

SOME OF THE MOST MEMORABLE AND POWERFULLY PROFOUND GATHERINGS WE'VE EVER HAD HAVE BEEN BECAUSE WE TOOK ONE OF THESE DETOURS OUTSIDE OUR LITURGY.

Some of the most memorable and powerfully profound gatherings we've ever had have been because we took one of these detours outside our liturgy.

One of the most wonderful things about meeting in your home and sharing life with your friends and family in Christ is that there's no "right way" or "wrong way" to be the Church together. All of your times together are sacred because Christ is in each of you and discovering Jesus in one another is actually more likely when you're not going through the familiar motions and rhythms of liturgy.

Step outside your comfort zone. Take a path less travelled and rediscover the thrill and joy of exploring your identity as the Body of Christ off the beaten path. You'll be glad you did!

DRAW OUT THE WALLFLOWERS AND REIGN IN THE SOAP BOXERS

In a truly new testament house church, no one person (or persons) do all the speaking and teaching. I do know of some organic churches who rely on one person, or sometimes a couple of people, to do all the teaching for them. However, it's my understanding that everyone in the Body of Christ has the freedom to share with everyone else in the gathering based on all the "one another" verses in the New Testament, and Paul's admonishment that "when you gather together one of you has a hymn, a tongue, a scripture," etc.

The challenge with the open share model of house church is that some people (like myself) have no problem talking at length about the Scriptures or their experience with God, while others are more shy or prefer to let others take the spotlight.

As a facilitator in our home church, my role has shifted from being the guy with all the answers to someone who limits themselves to no more than two soap box moments per meeting and spends most of the time trying to allow others to share their gifts as directed by the Holy Spirit.

In short, the less I talk the more opportunity I create for others to share from the heart and operate in their gifting to be a blessing to the rest of us. But, this takes practice and intention, and one of the most important exercises in this process is to start paying attention to those who are not talking. Look around the room and see if someone seems to have something on their mind, but isn't jumping into the conversation. Sometimes these people just need a little nudge, or an invitation from the group to share what's on their heart. Often in our group we'll stop and ask if there's anyone who wants to share something, especially if they're someone who hasn't spoken up in the group yet.

> THE LESS I TALK THE MORE OPPORTUNITY I CREATE FOR OTHERS TO SHARE FROM THE HEART AND OPERATE IN THEIR GIFTING TO BE A BLESSING TO THE REST OF US.

I believe that in every house church group there are those who are naturally teachers, some who are adept at providing color commentary to whatever someone else might share, and then there are those who rarely, if ever, speak, but when they do it's profound. Do whatever you can to draw out those who tend to hide in the shadows of the room and allow them to share more with everyone else. The more you demonstrate your love for their insight and appreciation of their thoughts and ideas, the more they'll feel comfortable sharing the next time you gather together.

There may even be times when you need to go privately to one or two individuals who seem to do most of the talking. Ask them to help you involve those who are on the sidelines more. Work together to wait before you speak and allow the uncomfortable silences to be filled by someone other than yourself once in a while. The results will be worth the effort, I believe.

LET JESUS BE THE LEADER

For the longest time, our house church family struggled with the idea of leadership. First, everyone looked to me because they considered me to be the pastor. Eventually I withdrew myself from this title and position and functionally encouraged everyone to step into their gifting and to take spiritual responsibility for one another as members of the priesthood of believers. But still, we weren't quite sure what it meant for Jesus to be the Head of our Church family.

I think every Christian would affirm the notion that Jesus is the head of their Church. However, in practice, the leader of the church is functionally the senior pastor. Of course, the assumption is that the senior pastor is hearing from Jesus and therefore the Church is being led by Jesus. But, according to Jesus himself, every believer is capable of hearing the His voice and responding to him. So, if all of us are able to hear the voice of Jesus, and if

Jesus is capable of speaking to us directly, why would we limit ourselves and allow only one specific person to hear the voice of Jesus on our behalf? Maybe we should all come together and practice listening to Jesus together each time we gather? Maybe Jesus is actually serious about leading us into all truth through the indwelling Holy Spirit? Maybe Jesus really can lead our times of worship, and prayer, and bible study if we actually ask him to? Maybe Jesus is powerful enough to teach us Himself? Maybe He actually wants to direct our time spent in His presence? Maybe Jesus actually does show up whenever two or more are gathered in his name?

If so, it makes a lot of sense for us to collaborate together as an organic body of disciples to surrender ourselves completely to the Lord Jesus Christ and allow Him to speak, and move, and minister, and touch, and encourage, and edify everyone in the room. How? Through us! We are his hands, his feet, and his children. We are filled and gifted by His Holy Spirit. We are empowered and called out to use our gifts to bless our brothers and sisters in the Church. But, it's not us doing the blessing, it's actually Jesus doing it as we surrender our will and our lives to His control.

Now, this isn't easy to do. It will take practice. It will involve praying together as a church family and asking Jesus to not only show up and lead you this way—but to help you as a group to learn how to respond to Him properly.

I can guarantee you that there will be times when someone speaks out of turn. There will be times when someone tramples on the Holy Spirit and does something, or says something, that is off base. Get used to that. But, don't give up! The more you submit to one another, and to Christ, in this process, the better you will get at learning to hear His voice and respond to His leadership and headship when you come together as a Body.

PLAN TO MULTIPLY INTO NEW GROUPS FROM DAY ONE

For a very long time now I've been of the opinion that our little house church is just too big. We've been hovering at around 28 people or so for the last few years now and this is just too many people to have a healthy and productive organic church, as far as I'm concerned. However, our house church is not a dictatorship, so I don't get to be the one who decides what we do or when we do it. I try to leave all of that up to God, and so far He's done a pretty good job of it.

For example, when we first started out our group only met on Thursday evenings. My family got together in our den every Sunday morning and shared together, but everyone else was at their home church on Sundays. After a while I really wanted to draw a line in the sand and force everyone on Thursday evenings to either come with us and commit themselves to us as a church that gathers on Sunday mornings, or hit the road. Luckily, God in his mercy gave me a very wise spouse. Wendy advised me to wait and to pray and see what God wanted to do. She reminded me that Jesus said that He would build His church and that He didn't really need my help doing it. Of course, if He did I would know it. Until then, we waited and we prayed.

Eventually, without any help from me, someone suggested that we start meeting on Sunday mornings, and suddenly people started calling the Mission their home church.

I share this because it reminds me that God really is in charge of His Church, not me. So, whenever I get antsy about the fact that our house church family feels too big I can remember that God can take care of these things without my intervention.

About a year ago two families left our group to start house church groups of their own. Again, without any help from me, both families decided that God was calling them to leave and start something in their home. Both families independently decided this on the same weekend. One went to Indiana, the other just up the road from us. Neither group asked for our permission but we all certainly gave them our blessing and we prayed over them to send them out.

Still, one thing that I wish I had done differently in our house church family was to communicate from day one to everyone that our hope and our plan was to keep the group small and to plant new house churches out of this one whenever we got too large to function properly as a family of believers. Not necessarily to create a benchmark number of people for this multiplication process, but simply to remind everyone involved that one of our goals as a church is to plant more churches out of this one. How we go about this, and when, is still up to God, but if your group starts out from the beginning with a clear understanding that this multiplication is part of the process, the easier it will be to actually plant new churches out of your group when the time comes.

> ONE THING THAT I WISH I HAD DONE DIFFERENTLY IN OUR HOUSE CHURCH FAMILY WAS TO COMMUNICATE FROM DAY ONE TO EVERYONE THAT OUR HOPE AND OUR PLAN WAS TO KEEP THE GROUP SMALL AND TO PLANT NEW HOUSE CHURCHES OUT OF THIS ONE WHENEVER WE GOT TOO LARGE

NO MASKS ALLOWED

One of the things I've loved the most about house church is that the home setting allows people to be themselves and communicate with one another without fear. At least, as long as you create an environment where people feel safe, that is. When people know that they can share doubts, fears, failures, and inconsistencies without being jumped on, attacked, treated differently, judged or pitied, they will eventually start to tell you the painful truth about themselves. This is where organic church really starts to get interesting.

Frankly, I have not been the first person to lead this trend in our house church family, but thankfully we've been blessed with a few people who just will not sit still for bullshit—and I love them for this.

One gentleman is constantly telling us how he doubts his faith or how he's not sure he really loves Jesus the way he should. This sort of thing makes most of us uncomfortable, and we will often spend some time trying to "fix" this person, but really this isn't why the person is sharing the truth with us. It's simply because he needs to speak the truth and he needs to know that there are people who are willing to hear it from him and still love him just the same.

I can remember leading a home group in our previous traditional church setting. Everyone in that group admitted that we didn't want to wear any masks. But in practice we all kept ours on and waiting for the person next to us to go first. Sadly, none of us really ever did. It wasn't until we got to the house church level that people felt comfortable admitting their sin, their weakness, their inadequacy, their fears, their doubts, their lack of faith, and their pain.

Several of my friends have come through the Twelve Step program at Alcoholics Anonymous, and from the conversations we've had about these kinds of meetings I can see that they've been practicing this kind of honesty for long, long time. I think I'd love to go with some of my friends when they go to their next meetings just so I can see for myself what a totally honest and open meeting is really like. This is how all of us should come together as a Body each week; we should show up admitting that we are weak and that we need help; we should confess to one another often just how screwed up and helpless we are to overcome our sins on our own; we should listen to one another without offering unsolicited advice and try to find ourselves in the other person's story without thinking of ourselves as being better or superior to them in any way.

If your group is still in the habit of pretending to have it all together, I must humbly suggest that you need to be the one to go first and take off your mask. Or, talk with your house church family about why your group doesn't feel safe enough to share what's really going on in your lives with one another. Ask some hard questions. Maybe even make a game out of it at first and go around the room sharing with one another your biggest doubts about your faith, or the most difficult thing about your walk with Christ.

> **IF YOUR GROUP IS STILL IN THE HABIT OF PRETENDING TO HAVE IT ALL TOGETHER, I MUST HUMBLY SUGGEST THAT YOU NEED TO BE THE ONE TO GO FIRST AND TAKE OFF YOUR MASK.**

The goal isn't to bring everyone down, but to take off the mask and get real enough with one another to start building one another up in the faith. We cannot do this if we never admit that we need building up. We cannot heal if we never show each other the wounds. We cannot comfort one another in our suffering is we never let anyone see us weep.

ROTATE LOCATIONS EARLY AND OFTEN

For the first 4 years of our house church life, our family hosted every meeting together. That's twice a week for four years! Today we only host twice a month (on Sundays) and other families take turns hosting in their homes the other weekends.

The reason we decided to rotate our meetings wasn't because we felt burnt out, however. Not at all. In fact, we really love hosting the house church in our home and it's very convenient for the kids on our street to join us on those Sundays, which makes it extra special for us. So, why did we decide to rotate our Sunday morning meetings? Well, it all started with a trip to Alaska. At least, an imaginary one.

As I've already mentioned, our house church group has been quite large for some time now. Over the last few years I've been pretty vocal about the fact that our group was too big and I really felt that there were plenty of mature people in our group who were more than capable of hosting and even leading a house church group in their own home. However, after a series of conversations and meetings with different people, what I learned was that none of those people saw themselves as ready, equipped or capable of doing this.

My epiphany came one evening when one of our brothers in the group asked everyone else this question: "If Keith and Wendy suddenly moved to Alaska next month, how many of you would even continue to meet together as a church every week?" To my surprise, and heartbreak, no one said that they would continue to meet together without our direct leadership in the group.

ANY CHURCH THAT CANNOT CONTINUE TO FUNCTION WITHOUT THE DIRECT LEADERSHIP OF THE LEADER ISN'T A CHURCH UNDER THE HEADSHIP OF CHRIST.

I think it was at this time that I recalled the words of wisdom shared by my friend Alan Knox who said that any church that cannot continue to function without the direct leadership of the leader isn't a church under the headship of Christ.

So, right then and there Wendy and I knew that we had failed to make disciples of the people in our house church. We wanted them to understand that they were all following Jesus—not us—and that He had equipped all of them to be the Church, and to be practicing members of the priesthood of Christ. That's when we started asking everyone in the group to step up and to start taking some of the responsibilities away from us and to start owning the group themselves. Sharing the weekly hosting duties was just one of the things we started to intentionally give away to the group. We also started not showing up to these meetings at all on occasion to underscore the reality that they could be the Church without any help from us at all.

The good news is that, about a year later, we asked some of these same people that question again about our mythical trip to Alaska and every one of them said that they would most definitely continue to meet with the house church family even if we were not there. I have to believe that hosting the house church meetings in different people's homes, and allowing everyone to experience the meeting apart from us made a difference. People got to see that there was nothing especially holy about our den, or about us as leaders, and that they were all called by God and empowered by the Holy Spirit to be the Body of Christ no matter where they gathered or who was in the room—or not.

CHAPTER 6

WHAT'S WRONG WITH ORGANIC CHURCH?

A few years ago, we hosted a conference in Southern California with Paul and Lori Byerly from House2House Ministries. During that meeting, we were asked to make a list of what's wrong with the house church movement, rather than focus on all the great things about it.

Specifically, we were tasked to look at how our brothers and sisters in the traditional church were better equipped than simple churches to handle certain tasks, and to contrast what they do well with areas where we sometimes struggle.

It was a refreshing break from our usual flag-waving, back-patting conversations and allowed us to really step back and take a look at ourselves and gain some much-needed perspective.

Here's what our list looked like:

- Organic churches are often invisible to the community

- Too inwardly focused

- Isolated from traditional churches

- Unequipped to deal with internal conflicts

- Too much spiritual pride—i.e. "We're doing it the right way"

- Lack of networking and connection with other house churches

- Too closed and secretive

- Reluctance to confront error, sin, in the Body—i.e. "Church Discipline"

- Lack of resources to deal with divorce, addiction, depression, etc.

In addition, we also identified perceived problems that our traditional brothers and sisters see in us:

- Perceived lack of strong leadership

- Lack of spiritual covering

- Prone to heretical doctrines and practices

Let's take some time to address these problems or weaknesses within the organic church.

INVISIBLE TO THE COMMUNITY

In our discussion we reflected on the fact that house churches don't have large signs out front, and don't market themselves the way traditional churches do. Because of this, it's often likely that a house church could exist for years right down the street from another house church and not even be aware of each other. Not to mention the fact that people in the community are also not aware that the house church meeting is taking place in their neighborhood.

So, what are the solutions to address this concern? I'd like to start out by isolating a few specific items first and addressing them individually.

HOUSE CHURCHES AREN'T AS GOOD AT MARKETING THEMSELVES AS TRADITIONAL CHURCHES ARE.

Why is this? One of the main reasons is that house churches are not, by nature, attractional model gatherings. That is, the point of a house church is not to attract or to gather as many people as possible each and every week. In fact, in our house church family, our goal is to gather with as small a group as possible every week. If our group were to suddenly have 20 new people start attending our gatherings every Sunday, we'd have to split our group into two or even three other smaller groups in order to continue to maintain the quality of our fellowship together.

Simply put, in the house church, bigger is not better. Now, that doesn't mean that we don't value evangelism. Our group just baptized 3 people last weekend, but this was after several months, even years, of relationship and discipleship over time.

SIMPLY PUT, IN THE HOUSE CHURCH, BIGGER IS NOT BETTER.

Here's the difference. In traditional churches I've served at in the past, our goal as a staff was to find new ways to attract a certain segment of people—young marrieds with children. We strategized ways to attract them. We flat out marketed our church to them with booths at local fairs and logo branded water bottles passed out at shopping malls and worship concerts in the park, etc. If we were successful we'd have 10 or 20 new people show up that Sunday morning and they'd eventually decide to join our church and tithe: *success*!

Now, with the house church it's almost completely upside-down from that. In our house church we prefer to meet regularly with other disciples of Jesus; people who are seriously trying to follow Jesus in their everyday life and who want to connect with others who simply want to learn how to put the teachings of Jesus into practice daily. We're not perfect. Far from it. If anything we know how weak we are and we know that, without the help of the Holy Spirit and the support of our church family, we'd never make it alone. If we kept on adding new people all the time we'd dilute our ability to share deeply with one another—because there are some things that you'll share with a group of five or six that you would never share in a group of 25 or 30 people. Also, if we were to grow too large too quickly, we would struggle to build relationships with one another and the quality of our community would suffer.

So, what do we do? Well, first of all we don't attempt to artificially increase the number of people who fellowship with us. At the same time, we do not attempt to eliminate people or turn anyone away who wants to join us. In essence, we do our best to let Jesus build His Church. And you know what? He does!

When our family first planted our house church we did not recruit anyone to come with us. Only one other family, and one single woman from our previous traditional church came with us (and only because they wanted to, not because we convinced them to). Everyone else who has ever come to our house church has found us, we have not found them.

Secondly, I want to address the issue of being invisible to the community we're planted in. To me, this is a more serious problem. We've always felt that our calling was not only to plant a house church in our home, but that God was planting a church in this specific neighborhood. In other words, we were here in this house because God had a plan (and He still does) to love the people on our street through us.

So, from the beginning, my family started reaching out to the kids in our neighborhood. At first that involved leading Kids Church in our home on Sunday mornings. Mainly because Wendy and I had been children's pastors at our previous church (and we loved teaching kids together), and also because by inviting the kids in our neighborhood to come on a Sunday morning we would figure out which families already went to church somewhere and which one's didn't. Most of them, we figured out, didn't attend anywhere on Sunday mornings.

Later, we hosted pancake breakfasts for everyone in our cul-de-sac on the Fourth of July and we intentionally went out of our way to meet our actual neighbors, invite them over for dinner, take out their trashcans for them, and serve them in whatever ways we could. In essence, we determined that we would become missionaries to our neighbors.

Over time, (and this is an ongoing story), we got to pray for families in real trouble. We got to encourage them. We got to share Jesus with their kids. We got to see their kids fall in love with Jesus. We got to share groceries with families in financial need. We got to tutor their kids in math and spelling. We got to babysit when they were in a bind.

Suffice it to say, our neighbors know that there's a church on their street, and they know that we love them and that Jesus loves them. We're still hoping to make a deeper impact for them and to bring the Kingdom of God into their lives in a more powerful way, but we also know that God wants this even more than we do and He will lead us as we continue to submit ourselves to Him.

TOO INWARDLY FOCUSED

One of the criticisms often hurled at those of us in the Organic Church is that we're too inwardly focused, and that we can become too closed or even secretive, preventing newcomers from entering into our little clique, or sometimes even scaring them away entirely.

Our little group isn't a closed group, and I don't think we're "secretive" or anything, but I have visited a few groups that were more inward-focused and there are a few things I'd like to say about this here.

IS IT TRUE?

I have to say that it's awfully hard to resist the temptation to be inwardly focused. I mean, no one has to be trained to be more inwardly focused. But we do need to constantly work at becoming more outwardly focused. It's a constant battle that we have to fight to take our eyes of ourselves and to look up to see the fields white unto harvest.

When my family first entered the wilderness to plant our little house church, it was primarily because we felt a strong calling from the Lord to plant a church where 100% of the offering could go to help the poor in the community. Because this was our goal, and our passion was to serve those who were trapped in poverty here in Orange County, California, we started a house church in order to allow all of the offering to be spent this way. Most house churches don't have such a story, and maybe that's why they tend to lean more towards isolation and inward-focused church life.

Being self-absorbed is an easy thing to do, really. The house church community is made up of people who, in many ways, feel like they're on the outside looking in when it comes to Christianity. Many of those who are attracted to house churches either have felt exploited by the traditional church, have felt a strong sense of unrest in the institutional church, or either feel called to explore a more organic form of church found in the New Testament. These factors can create a sense of being an outcast from other Christians, not to mention the world itself.

> THE HOUSE CHURCH COMMUNITY IS MADE UP OF PEOPLE WHO, IN MANY WAYS, FEEL LIKE THEY'RE ON THE OUTSIDE LOOKING IN WHEN IT COMES TO CHRISTIANITY.

I know many, many people involved in house churches now whose stories are filled with tales of lost friendships, damaged relationships with those in their previous traditional church who called them heretics, or who shunned them in grocery stores, or what have you.

These experiences are painful, and they are real. They also tend to create an isolationist mindset, because no one wants to get hurt in the same way again. Once you've found a like-minded group of Christians who can share your pain and who understand your grief at the loss of relationships in the church, it's easy to pull the shades, lock the doors and bask in the glow of those select few brothers and sisters who really "get you" and who understand where you're coming from, and where you're going.

I think the people who are part of our little house church family at the Mission are largely not the "hunker down" type. Some of us can indeed share stories about lost friendships, or church leaders who threatened or mocked us for pursuing the house church model. But, thankfully, we are not a group of wounded soldiers.

Most of us have been in leadership ourselves at the traditional churches we once attended. We've seen first-hand how broken the American version of Christianity can really be and we've made a conscious decision to move away from that top-down hierarchy model (of which we were once among the leaders), into a more shared version of church where members of the Body submit to one another and to Christ as our Head. At the same time, we know that it's important for us—as the Body of Christ—to "be the Church" to our community as well as in our regular weekly gatherings.

WHAT TO DO?

For those organic churches who are too inwardly-focused, and who are interested in becoming more outwardly-focused, I'd recommend a few things:

- Partner with another house church, or traditional church, to serve actual people in your community. Your goal is not to find a charity to write a check to. That's not going to change your inward focus into an outward focus. Look for ways to touch real human beings who need help, food, shelter, hope and the Gospel.

- Talk together about ways your group can serve the community. It doesn't have to be huge, either. Think simple. Maybe host a pancake breakfast in the neighborhood to start with, or visit a local senior home together with your kids once a month.

- Find a local charity, non-profit, rescue mission, etc. to volunteer at as a group.[1]

The goal of becoming more outwardly focused is not to lose your inward focus. There's nothing wrong with having an inward focus when you're together. That's called "community" and it's one of the primary strengths of the church. It's not that inward focus is bad, it's that not having any outward focus is tragic, and it's an incomplete picture of who we are called to be in Christ.

NOT HAVING ANY OUTWARD FOCUS IS TRAGIC, AND IT'S AN INCOMPLETE PICTURE OF WHO WE ARE CALLED TO BE IN CHRIST.

TOO SECRETIVE OR CLOSED?

I do know of a few house church groups that are closed; meaning that they do not accept any new people to visit or to join the fellowship. While our group isn't one of these kinds of groups, I must confess that I have secretly thought about starting just such a group myself. Why? Because there have been times when my family really wasn't getting as much out of our current house church experience as we needed to. Specifically, our two sons were not growing spiritually and my wife and I were also beginning to feel distant from the rest of the group. So, for a while we fantasized about leaving the church we started in order to gather with just one or two other families so we could really focus on going deeper with fewer people.

Eventually we changed our minds about that idea, but if we had decided to take such a step I don't think it would've been such a bad thing. I think, sometimes, there is a need to create a more intimate and intense space for people to pour into one another more directly. Although I'd quickly add that I think these sorts of groups should only be entered into seasonally, and that there should be an agreed upon expiration date for when the closed nature of the group will end and others will be welcomed into the fellowship. Perhaps this is where some groups fail? They start out with an inward focus to address specific needs of those within the group and then they just can't bring themselves to rock that boat and risk losing the good thing they've got going with one another. I don't know since I've never been part of a closed group like that myself. But I can see where the temptation to stay closed might come from.

EMBRACE THE MYSTERY

One thought I had when considering the secretive nature of the house church to those on the outside is that it might be possible to leverage this perceived secrecy in a positive way. I mean, if we're never going to advertise our house churches in the newspaper or on a billboard, or set up a big sign in our front yards, then why not go the other way? Why not play up the secretive part and use it to intrigue people into finding out more about why we meet in homes, and what we do there, and what makes it so different from everything else? People are naturally curious. What's wrong with appealing to their built-in desire to learn more? Especially if what people want to know more about is why you have to escape the man-made religious systems of the day in order to follow Jesus more and love your neighbor as yourself.

As followers of Jesus we are called to be set apart- to be different from the world around us. If being part of a house church creates an even greater opportunity for us to set ourselves apart from the world and to live different sorts of lives among others, we might as well make the best of it.

TOO ISOLATED FROM TRADITIONAL CHURCHES

It should be easy to understand why this problem persists. On one side you have Organic Churches made up of people who have left the traditional model, and on the other side you have traditional churches made up of people who see Organic

Churches as something of a threat, or at least an insult, to what they're doing. It's no wonder that these two groups don't often work together. But, I'd like to suggest that this shouldn't remain an acceptable condition in the Body.

There is only one Body, and there is only one Church. There are not House Churches and Traditional Churches, there is just one true ekklesia and different models of how this one church gathers and operates.

If we take this concept of "One Church" seriously, we must also take Jesus and Paul seriously when they instruct us to seek reconciliation and to live peacefully with all men. It really matters to God how we treat one another in the Body. This means that we cannot continue to remain in a place of animosity towards our brothers and sisters in the traditional church, or the ones in the organic church.

IT REALLY MATTERS TO GOD HOW WE TREAT ONE ANOTHER IN THE BODY.

God has been graceful to me in this matter. He has continually thrown me into relationship with pastors and leaders at traditional churches locally. This is not something I would have sought after on my own. And God knew this, so this is why He made sure that our little house church would end up partnering with Saddleback (a mega church) to plant an organic church at a motel in Santa Ana together. God is the one who opened a door for me to lead a men's bible study for a traditional church group each week. He has allowed me to pray regularly with a dear friend who is a local senior pastor of a large denominational church. Why? So that I could constantly be reminded that these people are my brothers and sisters. God loves them. They love God. They are seeking to follow Jesus too. We serve the same Lord. And our differences of modality should not prevent us from serving the poor together, or studying Scripture together, or praying for one another.

My story involves stepping away from an on-staff position at a local church that we helped to plant. It also involves leaving another church staff position where I was deeply invested emotionally. This wasn't done without some amount of pain and hurt feelings. But thankfully, God has allowed me to reconcile with the leaders of those churches I left. We still don't see eye-to-eye about church hierarchy or a business model of church, but we do love each other as brothers and we understand that loving one another is more important than anything else.

Eventually, I was asked to preach at the church I had left over 5 years previously. It was a huge blessing for me to return and to share some of what the Lord has been doing in my life. I was overwhelmed with their grace to me. They prayed over me for a half hour before the service. They embraced me at the end of the service. They even paid me a honorarium! None of this was expected, and frankly it would have never been possible if their senior pastor and myself hadn't gone out of our way to stay in touch, to reaffirm our love for one another, and to work hard at maintaining our friendship.

If you're unsure about it, let me assure you that God cares a whole lot about how we treat one another. The Greatest Command is that we love the Lord our God with all our heart, soul, mind and strength. The second greatest command, according to Jesus, "is like the first" and it is that we love our neighbor as ourselves. Why does Jesus say the second (love your neighbor) is "like the first" (loving God)? Because they are integrated concepts. "If anyone says he loves God and yet hates his brother, he is a liar" (1 John 4:20).

This is why Jesus also tells us that if we are at the altar and we remember that our brother has something against us, we are better off leaving our sacrifice on the altar and running quickly to reconcile with that brother and make sure that our hearts are right before God. (Matt 5:23-34)

Remember, God looks not at the outward appearance, nor does He measure our behaviors apart from examining our deeper motivations and ultimately our heart condition. So, it matters to God how we relate to one another, and especially how we love one another in the Church. And, again, there's only One Church. So, if you have something against a former pastor, or if you've shunned a brother or sister over disagreements about organic church or new testament models, (or any other reason), you really need to stop what you're doing and seek for reconciliation and peace, "as far as it depends on you."

If we are truly Kingdom-minded churches, then we will not ever decide to without love or fellowship or assistance from another Christian because they disagree with us doctrinally or belong to another expression of church.

UNEQUIPPED TO DEAL WITH INTERNAL CONFLICTS

What do you do when someone in your house church family is unrepentantly walking in sin? How do you respond? Do you just ignore it and hope it will go away? Do you talk about it behind their back with others in the group? Or, do you quietly pray for them and keep it to yourself because you feel uncomfortable with confrontation?

Frankly, most Christians tend to gossip about, ignore or avoid the sin of others in their church—house church or otherwise. Mainly because we don't like to get into other people's business, and because we just don't like the idea of confronting sin in others.

Now, I know from experience that any discussion like this will inevitably lead to discussions about judging others and casting the first stone, or the plank in your own eye. I'm not talking about creating a legalistic, judgmental atmosphere in your church family. We need to have grace for one another and there is room for maturity over time on certain issues, but when someone in the church body is having sex outside of marriage, or committing adultery, or abusing drugs or alcohol, or otherwise damaging their witness and slandering the name of Christ by their actions, we do have a Biblical mandate to lovingly correct such behavior.

Both Jesus and Paul outline a clear series of steps towards reconciliation and restoration of a brother or sister trapped in sinful activity. The goal of this process is always restoration. The tone and the spirit of the process is always deep, sincere love and integrity. Church discipline, if it's done properly, should always be entered into with tears and the aim should always be to bring the person back into full and complete fellowship with the Body of Christ.

Here's what Jesus teaches us about how to handle conflict in the Church:

> "If your brother sins against you, go and tell him his fault, between you and him alone. If he listens to you, you have gained your brother. But if he does not listen, take one or two others along with you, that every charge may be established by the evidence of two or three witnesses. If he refuses to listen to them, tell it to the church. And if he refuses to listen even to the church, let him be to you as a Gentile and a tax collector. Truly, I say to you, whatever you bind on earth shall be bound in heaven, and whatever you loose on earth shall be loosed in heaven. Again I say to you, if two of you agree on earth about anything they ask, it will be done for them by my Father in heaven. For where two or three are gathered in my name, there am I among them." (Matthew 18:15-20)

This passage deals, specifically, with how we should handle interpersonal conflict in the Church ("If a brother sins against you"), but it's a perfectly good process for handling the restoration of fellowship with someone in the Church family who is unrepentantly continuing in sin. Notice the first step is to go privately to the person in the hopes of restoring fellowship. If this isn't successful we are told to take "one or two others" with us—again with the hope of restoring right fellowship between members of the Body of Christ. The goal is not to shame anyone. It's not to point out their sinful failures. It's simply, from the very beginning, about seeking peace between members of God's family and bringing someone back into right relationship with Christ. The very last step is to take it to the Church body. This final step, again, is to be done with an eye towards hopeful restoration of the person's dignity and fellowship. It should be done with tears and with a sincere desire to bring this person back into the fullness of Christ. It's only if all of these steps fail that anyone should be removed from the community of faith.

IT'S SIMPLY, FROM THE VERY BEGINNING, ABOUT SEEKING PEACE BETWEEN MEMBERS OF GOD'S FAMILY AND BRINGING SOMEONE BACK INTO RIGHT RELATIONSHIP WITH CHRIST.

Why should we employ this process in the church? Because we're protecting not only this person's spiritual health, we're also concerned about the message they are sending to the world about what it means to be a follower of Jesus. Paul is especially clear about this aspect of protecting the witness of Christ in one another when he urges the church to deal with error and sin in their midst. (see 1 Cor 5: 1-13)

Church Discipline is necessary because it's not only important to help one another follow Christ with integrity, it's also important that we stand up and together to more faithfully define for those outside the Body what a true follower of Jesus looks like.

Someone who openly lives in disobedience to the clear example of Christ is not a true follower of Jesus, and if we will not point this out to the world, then who will?

Over the years, our house church family has only had to confront these sorts of things a few times. Only once did it come to asking someone not to return to the group, but in that case it was only until we could verify some disturbing information from another church about this person's past history. Specifically, this person's previous pastor provided some information that appeared to show that this person had lied to us, taken money from the church under false pretenses and was avoiding a host of addiction-related issues. I offered to meet with him privately at a time and place of his choosing until we could sort it all out. He nearly took a swing at me, but declined my offer to talk this out and never returned.

I wish I could tell you that we've always handled this process perfectly, but sometimes we've had to learn from our mistakes in this area. Thankfully, no one was damaged as a result of our foolishness and we continue to remain in good fellowship with everyone involved. (Except this person in the above example, although I did run into him about a year later and he embraced me and prayed for me and said that everything was much better now…so, I guess even this one worked out too, by the Grace of God).

So, whether you're part of a house church, or an organic church, the need for church discipline remains, and it's commanded by our Lord Jesus.

The major difference in the organic church is that church discipline is done by the Body, and out of relationship, not through an external or artificial hierarchy. Even Jim Belcher, local pastor and author of Deep Church, agrees that hierarchical structures aren't necessarily capable of bringing about true repentance.

About a year ago I was interviewed by Jim Belcher for his book, and in it he references our discussion in two different chapters, touching on this very issue, saying:

> "My greatest concern about house churches like Keith Giles's is that there is no formal structure for discipline. When I asked him how he would mediate a struggle between him and another member or leader…he really did not know. He would try, he said, to convince that person based on the strength of their relationship. But I have seen firsthand that this is not always enough. Sometimes a higher court, like an elder board or a denomination is needed."

Although Belcher sees a need for a denominational authority in these cases, he goes on to agree with my assertion that relationships are more powerful than hierarchy when it comes to addressing these concerns:

> "Keith would agree that they have no hierarchy, offices and fluid structures. But he would disagree that they have no accountability. When I asked about discipline, he said it is done through the relationships that are built in the house church. He mentioned a few times that he has had to confront wrong choices people have made.
>
> 'If they are not going to listen to me, when I love them,' he said, 'why would they listen to someone above me in a hierarchy?'
>
> I would have to agree." (Jim says)

In the actual interview between Belcher and myself, he went on to share several very specific instances where he personally confronted people in his church who were behaving sinfully and they did not waver when he brought in the denominational authority.

Still, the issue of church discipline in an organic church can be a tricky thing. Mainly because most of us do not like conflict or confrontation, and if we're going to respond to sin in our midst, or correct someone who is teaching something heretical, we're going to have to do more than a little confronting.

Another friend of mine, Todd Hunter (now a Bishop in the Anglican church), once told me that the condition of the person's heart is actually more of a determining factor in these cases than anything else, saying, *"A good man will remain faithful, even with a poor structure of accountability, and a degenerate man will frustrate and resist even the most iron-clad system of accountability."* I must agree.

So, while it may be one of the more difficult aspects of participating in an organic church, discipline within the Body is still a necessary part of growing in community with one another.

LACK OF NETWORKING WITH OTHER HOUSE CHURCHES

When I first started hosting a house church in our home, about five years ago now, I was desperate to connect with others who were doing the same thing we were. Mainly just so I wouldn't feel all alone, and so I could learn from the mistakes of others without making them all on my own.

One of the first people I got in touch with was Ken Eastburn of The Well. We started out meeting at a local Carl's Jr. and over time we developed a friendship that continues to this day. Ken's story was not the same as mine. He was the pastor of a local Baptist church that transitioned into a series of house churches after selling their building. Still, Ken and I were able to encourage one another and inspire each other to continue on in our journey into New Testament church.

Out of the many ideas we bounced around together, one of them was to create a network of local house churches in the Orange County area. We both knew the value of getting connected with others who were hearing the same call on their life and sharing stories, ideas and resources with one another. From here we added other local house church leaders and advocates like Bill Faris and Michael Bischoff.

Of course, not every house church wants to connect with others in this movement. I've had some people over for dinner who were hosting house churches locally who had no interest in meeting others, or in connecting with other house churches. I'm not sure why this is, but I do know from experience that it's so much better to have people you can reach out to for ideas, for encouragement, for prayer and for support as you walk down this organic church experience. Not only that, I think there's a biblical precedence for this networking together of churches. In the New Testament there were no maverick groups. Every house gathering in a city was considered as one church family. Paul letters to the church in Corinth, the church in Galatia, the church in Ephesus, the church in Collosse. He did not write to individual groups, or to pastors. He wrote to everyone who was in that city or region as one church family.

So, there's one church in Orange County, made up of house churches, and traditional churches, of all denominations and practices. We are the church in Orange County, and the more we get to know and to love one another, and to work together to preach the gospel, to feed the poor, and to advance the Kingdom of God in Orange County, the better.

Now, with a house church the idea of finding everyone is difficult, as we've already discussed in this series. House Churches don't have signs out front or ads in the paper. Some have blogs or websites, but not all of them do. Some are closed groups for example and the last thing they want is to attract newcomers. So, getting connected with other house church and simple church groups in your area can be a challenge. But, that doesn't mean you shouldn't try!

One good place to start is over on Facebook. There are several great groups like one that I help to moderate called "Organic Church Movement", and several others. You can list your house church group and also search for the groups that are nearest to you.

Remember: you don't need to agree with everything the other groups practice. Ken Eastburn and I are like night and day on most things, and both of us are different from Bill Faris and Mike Bischoff, but we still meet regularly for lunch, share ideas, encourage one another and even hose monthly "OC/Organic Church Forums" where people can come to meet with others in the local organic church movement, and to discuss important topics, share ideas, etc.

I'd encourage you do all you can to connect with others in your area who may be leading or participating in house church. If you're all alone in the desert, I'd suggest connecting online at Facebook or try Googling for "Organic" or "House Church" or "Simple Church" in your area.

The organic church is especially relational, so the more we stay in relationship with others the more we can learn and the more we can work together to have an impact on our community for Christ.

LACK OF STRONG LEADERSHIP

This criticism of organic church comes from those outside the movement, not from those within. Mainly because the perception of what leadership should look like differs from what most of us have come to expect in the traditional church setting.

When I was a pastor on staff at a traditional church I was seen as a leader. This meant my success was literally measured by how many people were following me and, more importantly, how good I was at getting them to do the things around the church that needed to be done. In my case this was either serving the poor in one of our regular outreach events, teaching Sunday School on Sunday mornings, attending a youth event, or showing up for choir practice.

As a leader I was expected to read books on leadership, to attend pastor conferences where leadership skills could be developed, and to target those in our church who had leadership potential and recruit them for my particular ministry.

In a traditional context, a good leader is charismatic, inspirational, and motivational. He or she is graded on how many people respond to instructions and perform the desired activity.

In an organic church all of this is thrown right out the window. I once described it this way to someone who didn't understand what leadership was like in an organic church. I said, "instead of a top-down, CEO-style leader like we're used to seeing, imagine someone on their knees with a towel around their waist who is washing someone's feet."

Jesus is our model for leadership in the organic church, and frankly it's much, much harder to emulate his example than it is to just take charge and tell everyone what to do.

A SUCCESSFUL LEADER IN THE ORGANIC CHURCH, OR THE NEW TESTAMENT EKKLESIA, IS MEASURED NOT BY HOW MANY PEOPLE FOLLOW THAT LEADER, BUT BY HOW MANY PEOPLE ARE FOLLOWING CHRIST DUE TO THAT PERSON'S INFLUENCE. THERE IS A DIFFERENCE.

A successful leader in the organic church, or the New Testament ekklesia, is measured not by how many people follow that leader, but by how many people are following Christ due to that person's influence. There is a difference.

As someone who spent a few decades learning how to be good at being up front and telling people what to do and think, this new servant model was much more challenging for me. And it still is.

When our house church group first started, I used to answer every question that was asked in our share time. Mainly because whenever anyone asked a question every eye would turn to me in expectation. Everyone saw me as the leader, the expert, and I was only too ready to demonstrate my expertise. Partly because this is how I was trained, and partly because I'm a little bit proud and being seen and treated as the resident expert on the Bible made me feel important.

One Sunday morning when one of our members asked a question about a passage we were discussing together I took a different approach. She said, "What does this verse mean?" and instead of answering I sat back and said, "I don't know. Does anyone else here have an idea?" And after that I did everything in my power to give away the spotlight to the rest of the Body.

Usually I allow someone else to play the guitar during our singing times, but lately I'm the only person who feels comfortable doing this for our group. The problem this created for us was that it put me in the front of the room and after the singing everyone was left staring at me, once again, in expectation of what I was going to do or say to lead our group. To counteract this I used to play the last song and then, while everyone's eyes were still closed, I would get up and leave the room. When people opened their eyes I wasn't sitting there and it forced the group to take responsibility for the share time without looking to me for guidance. I would only return to the group after I heard them talking from the next room, usually carrying my second cup of coffee, or a book I wanted to read from.

If anything, leadership in a house church context is more about what you *don't* do, and the goal is to facilitate the group to function and grow apart from your constant oversight. There have even been meetings where I'm not even there! Usually those are the best meetings of all, I say.

Leadership as Jesus modelled for us was not top down, it was bottom up. He always found ways to ask the right questions, to recognize the people on the fringes, and to model a radical form of service to those he was leading. Jesus was a master at leaving hard questions unanswered and asked hard questions of his own in order to help people work out the answers they were seeking. Even though he was full of knowledge, even though his disciples desperately wanted him to just tell them what to do and how to think, he continually kept them mentally and spiritually engaged by always giving them some other mystery to work out, or some new concept to explore.

I am not like Jesus. Not yet. I mean, I really wish that I was, but the truth is that I'm still learning how to let go of my authority and position and to help others to grapple with His Word and to be lead by His Spirit as they follow Jesus daily.

Certainly, I do have something to contribute to the church family that God has made me part of, but I do not have all the answers. I have part of the message, but according to the New Testament, God will lead each of us by His Spirit and has already gifted everyone in our fellowship with the gifts they need to be a blessing to others in our fellowship. The ministry of the Body is found in the Body, and not in me or any other expert. Allowing Christ to be the Head of His Church and to lead us whenever we gather together is not always easy, but it does require much more faith and a lot of grace for one another as we learn how to share and to serve one another in His love.

TOO PROUD OF OURSELVES

I've saved this one for last because, honestly, it's probably the one area where I've failed the most miserably. It's also the one area where pretty much every person who embraces simple church has fallen victim to their own excitement—at least once.

When I first discovered the New Testament model of church I was so excited on the one hand (about how plainly the scriptures supported what we were doing) and so angry (that for so long I had been blind to these things) that I had to shout it from the mountaintops—or at least from the top of my blog—for all to hear.

One friend who felt especially insulted and defensive about my overzealous articles told me later—at a lunch meeting where we both did plenty of apologizing to one another—that my rapid fire, non-stop blasting of the traditional church model was so overwhelming for him that he felt that his only recourse was to escalate the discussion to the nuclear option. In effect, I left him no room for concession and my approach was so provoking and ungracious that he couldn't have a friendly dialog with me over the issue. Hence the need for a make-up lunch meeting where we could both apologize, bury the hatchet and reaffirm our friendship.

> I'VE OFTEN SAID THAT THE BEST WAY TO TALK TO OTHERS ABOUT THE WONDERS OF THE SIMPLE CHURCH EXPERIENCE IS TO FOCUS ON THE BLESSINGS, THE GOOD FRUIT THAT COMES FROM THIS NEW TESTAMENT-INSPIRED IDEOLOGY.

I've often said that the best way to talk to others about the wonders of the simple church experience is to focus on the blessings, the good fruit that comes from this New Testament-inspired ideology. Like bringing warm bread out of the oven, the smell fills the house and everyone stops what they're doing to say, "Mmm… that smells great! Can I have some of that?"

Sadly, I've only recently learned how to apply this philosophy in my writing about organic church. And some people will still find ways to be offended or threatened by my writing no matter what tone I take or how much I attempt to be gracious. Still, as long as I do my part to share the story in love there's nothing I can do about how people respond.

This is partly why this book about the Church took over 3 years to finish. The first and second drafts were essentially collections of my previous articles on the subject and most of those were intentionally provocative and agitating in their tone. You see, I used to believe that the best way to get noticed, and to have your articles shared and talked about, was to write the most incendiary and controversial article possible in order to wake people up and shake them into action. In some ways this strategy did work. I did get lots of comments, and I did generate a lot of reaction. But sadly, the only result was that those who already agreed with me felt justified to be just as confrontational as I was, and those who did not agree with me were only pushed further away from any possibility of taking me, or my ideas, to heart.

This is why I started my book over from scratch after over 2 years writing, re-writing and editing. I knew that the people I wanted most to read the book and to consider my ideas would never make it past the introduction if I kept such an adversarial tone. So, I painfully scrapped my nearly-completed 250 page draft and started over from the beginning. My hope was to ask potential skeptics to give me some grace and to take a look at some amazing scriptures about what God's plan for His Church has been from the beginning of time. Even if they didn't draw the same conclusions as I did, at least it might be possible to show them—as my brothers and sisters in Christ—a little more detail about the New Testament temple than they've probably ever realized before.

Of course, I do understand that the implication of what I propose can seem threatening to someone whose entire career has been built upon full-time ministry through tithes and offerings at a denominational church. And I can totally understand why someone in that position might not want me to spread such concepts around so freely. But, hopefully I can at least communicate the wonders of God's awesome plan for His people in a way that intrigues and inspires them to see themselves through the eyes of a Creator who loves them and has made plans to draw near to them as they realize who they are in Christ and actually begin to function as a true Body under the divine leadership of Jesus, the true vine.

This criticism about organic church practitioners being too proud and arrogant is, sadly, one we must own and perhaps also seek to change in order to invite more people to consider our oh-so-valid perspectives on ekklesia and organic church life.

CHAPTER 7

ANSWERING QUESTIONS ABOUT HOUSE CHURCH

Here are some of the common questions and concerns raised about house church and a look at what we've done in our community at The Mission to address them.

WHAT ABOUT THE KIDS?

Usually this question is the very first one we hear. Most people can't imagine juggling little Billy while they pray for someone or engage in meaningful dialog about the gifts of the Spirit. Others are asking because they fear being the one elected to spend the two hours at house church alone in a guest room with six toddlers and a fussy baby while everyone else enjoys the fellowship and community in the living room.

At our house church we have invited the children to be with us throughout the entire gathering. They are the Church too so we allow them to share and speak and pray and participate along with everyone else. In fact, the children are usually the very first to speak up and share a scripture verse with the group. What's more, their insights often lead our discussions into challenging territory.

"At that time Jesus said, 'I praise you, Father, Lord of heaven and earth, because you have hidden these things from the wise and learned, and revealed them to little children. Yes, Father, for this was your good pleasure.'" (Matt 11:25-26)

We do have little toddlers who either play quietly on the floor under the supervision of their parents, or play in the other room with a parent nearby if they are fussy or disruptive. However, for the most part we tolerate children being children. We do not view the gathering and share time as a performance that needs to be "just so" and this means we're not offended when a kid laughs or talks out loud or whatever. Many of us are parents too and we have grace for one another.

After about an hour or so, the kids tend to get restless so we usually dismiss them to go watch videos in the other room or to play outside in the back yard while the adults move into more serious talk and/or prayer and ministry time.

WHAT ABOUT NON-PROFIT STATUS FOR THE TAX WRITE-OFF?

The next most important question (if not the first) is always money. Many are used to receiving a Giving Statement from their Church so they can write it off their taxes. I'm sure there are a few people who don't attend our house church because of the simple fact that we do not provide this service to them, however we felt a strong conviction against filing for Non-Profit Status and here two reasons why:

1. We give out of simple compassion and obedience. The gift is about helping others. It is not about us.

   An example I always use is something like this: If you were walking down the street and ran into a homeless woman who was cold and sick and hungry on the sidewalk, would you say, "Wait here while I go find an appropriate Non-Profit organization where I can give my money (so that I can get a tax write-off) and then I'll be right back with clothes and food to help you." I hope not.

2. We do not want the Government to have any control or say over what we do or say. We do not need the State of California's approval to meet or to worship or to follow Jesus. We are the Church.

Of course, others feel differently and if they depend on the tax write-off for their family finances I simply encourage them to give to another non-profit of their choice.

HOW SHOULD WE HANDLE THE OFFERING?

We do not pass the basket in our church. We do not mention the offering as part of our ongoing conversation, except once in a while I might announce that we are helping someone who is need and/or send out a regular statement of how our offering has been invested in the lives of the poor in our community.

WE TAKE OUR ATTITUDE TOWARDS THE OFFERING FROM THE EARLY CHURCH AND GIVE 100% OF OUR OFFERING BASKET MONEY TO THE POOR.

We take our attitude towards the offering from the Early Church and give 100% of our offering basket money to the poor. I do not take a salary and we do not use any of that money for food, rent, utilities, dessert, etc. All of it goes to help people in need, both inside and outside our house church family.

We are also 100% transparent with all of the money we receive each week and where and how it is spent each week. The ongoing log or book is kept in the same basket where the money is received so anyone, at any time, can see what's going on with the money.

One year we were amazed to discover that our little house church had given over $3,000 to the poor in our community. The next year we would go over that amount.

Why? Because when people can see that the $100 they gave went to help someone pay their bills or feed their children or make it through another week they start to get excited about giving. They truly become "Hilarious givers" who take joy in providing help to others. Imagine that...

WHAT DOES IT MEAN TO "BE THE CHURCH?"

Those of us who are part of a house church or an organic church often speak of "being the church" rather than "attending a church."

A fellow house church leader recently emailed me and a few other house church practitioners to ask us how we would answer this question: *"How are your house church communities doing at 'being the Church' rather than 'going to Church'?"*

Here's my response: Over the last few weeks I've had conversations with several in our house church family and they've indicated to me that they've started to experience a paradigm shift between "going to church" and "being the church." Here's how some of them have expressed this phenomenon:

- "Once I realized that being who God created and called me to be was all that He expects of me, I started to realize that I have a ministry to children already. I don't have to travel to Africa or even to Mexico to minister to children who don't know the Gospel. They're in my 5th grade class I teach every day."

- "I had only been coming to this house church for two weeks when I offered to host the next meeting in my home. Everyone was like, 'That's great!' At first I thought, 'Don't you want to see my house first?' but then I realized that it didn't matter to anyone what my house was like. They were all eager to allow me the freedom to contribute to the Church in whatever way I wanted to."

- "All my life at other churches I was always on the outside of that mysterious inner circle of leadership, but now I'm one of the many other contributing members of the Church. Suddenly my voice counts for something. My gifts are relevant. My family is truly known and loved. This is what Church is all about!"

- "Growing up in Church I never understood what the pastor was saying. But now I'm free to ask questions and people are free to question me and to challenge me in my walk with Jesus. It's the Body of Christ that has changed my life where all those sermons never did."

- "For the first time in my life as a Christian, when I think of "my church," I now think of the people in it. Not the building or the pastor because we don't have any. The faces of the people I fellowship with come to mind."

- "Instead of going to church and attending a meeting, the house church experience has allowed me to see that all of my life is a ministry to God. No matter where I am or what I'm doing, the Spirit of the Living God is alive in me and that's where 'Church' can happen."

Our house church is called "the Mission" because we hope to encourage everyone to see that they are missionaries equipped by God to minister the Gospel in their own neighborhood, workplace, community, etc.

In addition to these statements, I've personally witnessed individuals in our house church family as they discover their own personal mission. Some have felt a calling to start a weekly prayer meeting in their home. Some have felt compelled to take regular trips to an orphanage in Mexico. Some have taken it upon themselves to put together survival kits for the homeless. Some have responded to God's calling to use their teaching gift to lead weekly Bible Studies with people outside our house church family. Some have stepped out to help teach Chinese students how to speak English as a second language. Others are still trying to understand what their personal mission is and we're patiently standing by them and encouraging them as they continue to follow Jesus daily.

While no one in our house church family feels pressure to participate in anyone else's ministry, they do know that they are free to join in if they want to. No one feels pressure to start a ministry of their own either. Unless God is genuinely speaking to them about stepping forward, we're content to meet them wherever they are.

Our house church family has a saying that goes, *"We're all in process."* That means we recognize that none of us is in exactly the same place in our walk with Christ. While we encourage everyone to grow deeper with Jesus, we don't set our own expectations of what that should look like. We allow the individual person to listen for God's voice and to respond accordingly. We strive to have grace for one another and not to impose our passion on others.

For example, my family has been serving at a local motel for many years now. We go every month and pass out free groceries which our house church family purchases using the offerings that are freely given to help the poor. Not everyone in our house church goes with us when we serve at the motel, but they know we'd love to have them join us if they wish. They also know that they don't have to give their offering to this cause if they don't want to. No one forces them to give or looks to see who is giving or how much. We don't impose our vision and mission on them and they don't try to convince us that their personal ministry should be everyone else's.

> RATHER THAN EXPLOIT ONE ANOTHER TO BENEFIT OUR MINISTRY, WE EMPOWER ONE ANOTHER TO STEP OUT AND SERVE OTHERS IN WHATEVER WAY WE FEEL CALLED.

Rather than exploit one another to benefit our ministry, we empower one another to step out and serve others in whatever way we feel called. We help when we can. We encourage one another, and we cheer each other onward.

So, in a nutshell this is how our little house church family is learning to "be the Church" to one another and to people we come into contact with each and every day.

HOW DO YOU LEAVE YOUR TRADITIONAL CHURCH WITH GRACE?

I received this email below from someone who had a question after reading this book.

"Hi Keith,

I've been on a journey for the last two years or so as I work out what organic New Testament Christianity looks like.

There is one thing I am wrestling with that I hope you can help me process: How does one leave a traditional church gracefully, without losing the relationship of genuine spiritual mothers and fathers? While I may not agree with the model of church that they subscribe to, my issue is not with them personally as believers. These are people who have laughed and cried with me and encouraged me to pursue the dreams God has placed on my heart. I'm now convinced of the need for Christians to gather in a more organic way like a house church setting, but equally convinced that there has to be a better way to do this than just telling my church "You guys have got it wrong. I've found a better way. See ya!"

Does that make sense?"

I believe this is a common question that many struggle with. Here's my answer:

First of all, when it's time for you to go you'll know it. The pain of staying will be greater than the pain of leaving to pursue a more organic form of New Testament church.

But, when you do leave, be sure to leave well. As it says:

"If possible, so far as it depends on you, be at peace with all men." (Romans 12:18)

Just so you know, it might not be possible to leave without a few hurt feelings, especially on the part of your pastor and leadership staff. They will most likely see your exit as a betrayal and as a criticism of their ministry no matter how hard you try.

Even so, make sure to bless them on your way out. They may not bless you, but you need to bless them.

> EVEN SO, MAKE SURE TO BLESS THEM ON YOUR WAY OUT. THEY MAY NOT BLESS YOU, BUT YOU NEED TO BLESS THEM.

To do this, ask the Lord to give you love and mercy and grace for them, even as they mock you and shun you and slander you behind your back. Consider this is an exercise in sharing in the sufferings of Christ.

Also, remember that you are not "leaving the church" because the Church is the Body of Christ (all over the world). Yes, you are choosing not to fellowship with a specific group of Christians in a certain place and time, but you are not leaving Christ—therefore you are not leaving His Church.

This also means that you are still a member of those people. They are still your brothers and sisters, and you should treat them as such even after you step away from that fellowship. In other words, don't break the bond of love, even if you break the bond of weekly fellowship.

Now, I have to ask, "What are you leaving for?" I mean, where are you going next? Are you looking to start a house church in your community? Are you looking to join an existing group? What's next? Where is the Lord leading you?

This is just as important as "How do I leave?" because you have to know what it is that God is leading you to go and do next. Even if all you know is that you're going to pursue a more open meeting where every believer is free to participate and share according to their gifting, you still have to have some idea of what comes next.

Finally, just remember, you are not alone. There are hundreds and thousands of other Christians who have made this same step.

If you're not already part of a house church community, I'd suggest joining a few Organic Church groups on Facebook.

The important thing is to move closer to Jesus in this process, and to move closer to the Body life experience that you know is part of God's plan for you and your family. Don't walk away from one fellowship into a vacuum. That's probably even worse than staying where you are.

IS A STATEMENT OF FAITH NECESSARY FOR UNITY?

Let's suppose you have a family in our house church that has been with you for several years. They laugh with you, cry with you, worship with you and serve with you on a daily basis. You've heard the Lord speak to you profoundly through these dear people. Their family is part of your family. You cannot imagine being a church without them.

However, imagine now that they do not fully embrace the doctrine of the Trinity. Let's say they believe that Jesus is God, but that he also takes the form of the Holy Spirit and sometimes the Father. [It's called the "Jesus Only" or "Oneness" doctrine for those of you who are not familiar with the concept.]

Although they do not agree with you or anyone else in your church family about the Trinity, they also never attempt to argue for their "Jesus Only" view or impose their perspective on anyone else in the church. What do you do? Do you invite them to leave? Do you host an intervention and attempt to show them how wrong they are?

As I was reading Rad Zdero's latest book, "*Letters to the House Church Movement,*" I found myself asking myself this very question. What would I do? In his book, Zdero provides a specific example of an occasion when he counseled a family to separate themselves from another family they had been serving with for a long time because of just such a difference regarding the Trinity doctrine. But, is that the right thing to do? I'm not so sure.

So, let me share with you my thoughts on this idea of formalizing our beliefs into a statement of faith.

First of all, let me affirm that I am a Trinitarian. I do accept the traditional Christian view that God is One being who is revealed in three separate persons as the Father, the Son and the Holy Spirit. However, is this view something that we should use a litmus test for fellowship, or even for salvation in Christ?

Jesus did not seem to believe that it was of utmost importance that the Disciples/Apostles understand the doctrine of the Trinity. If He did, then He did not stress it to them in His teachings anywhere. Also, the Apostles and the NT church did not ever seem to be of the opinion that agreement with this doctrine be the litmus test for salvation. Again, if they did then we should see some very strong teaching in that regard. And we don't.

Yes, I do believe the doctrine of the Trinity, but I also believe that salvation is by Grace, through faith alone in Christ Jesus. That means when an 8 year old girl prays to receive the Christ as Lord and Savior and begins to follow Him, we do not automatically expect her to be capable of explaining the Trinity to anyone. If she fails to explain the Trinity correctly do we proclaim that she is not saved? I wouldn't think so. So, I'm of the opinion that it's better to allow people to grow in their understanding of who Christ is and not dismiss people for not being where I want them to be doctrinally.

I think my response is also tempered by the fact that our house church is made up of people from a wide variety of backgrounds: Baptist, Methodist, Brethren, Charismatic, Presbyterian, Vineyard, Calvary Chapel, Pentecostal, etc. Because of this wide diversity we have maintained our love for one another and our unity by simply not allowing any particular theological perspective to rise above the over-arching practice of learning how to follow Jesus in our daily lives and how to love Him and love one another as He commands us.

Do we disagree on doctrine? Yes! But not intentionally, and certainly not during our fellowship time together. Exceptions to this rule are few, of course, but in general we try to focus our time on Jesus and allowing His Spirit to lead us. Sometimes our differing perspectives leak out, but in those cases we are all careful to express those differences with grace. For example, one brother in our fellowship is a dispensationalist. I am not. Most of us are not, actually. So, if our perspective of a particular verse is informed by that doctrine we say, "I believe XYZ because of the way I understand these verses ABC." We try to allow for the possibility that we could be wrong, and we allow others to voice their different view if they want to. But the key is that none of us is attempting to impose our views on anyone else. We share our perspectives openly, but we do not divide on those issues— and we never allow those differences to overshadow our time together in Christ.

EVERYONE IS IN PROCESS

As I've said before, we the way we respond to our differences is by acknowledging that "we are all in process" and by that I mean that we all fully admit that there are convictions we hold today that we did not hold five years ago. We also know that the convictions we hold now could change in the next five years. We are all in process, and because of that we have grace for one another and we do not try to harvest green fruit or coerce people to agree with our perspective.

As you might have guessed, our house church does not have any formalized statement of faith. Whenever someone comes to our church and expresses a desire to join with us we simply say, "If you love Jesus and if you're sincerely trying to follow Him in your daily life, you're in!" That's it. If people aren't comfortable with this, they usually excuse themselves. (And some have, but not because we invited them to leave).

Here's one reason why we have not attempted to write any sort of Statement of Faith for our house church: Historically, every time the Church has tried to bring unity through the writing of doctrines it has always resulted in greater division because some will always disagree with that doctrine. Doctrinal statements have never resulted in increased unity, only increased division. That's why we allow people to grow in their understanding of Christ and of the Scriptures at their own pace.

OLLY OLLY OXEN FREE?

Does that mean there are no standards? Of course not. None of us would allow an outsider, or an insider for that matter, to introduce a teaching that was contrary to clear Biblical truth. For example, if someone came and wanted to convince us that Jesus was a space alien from Alpha Centauri, or the spirit-brother of Lucifer, we would all open our Bibles and demonstrate that Jesus is no such thing. The key, of course, is that none of us attempts to sway anyone else in our group to agree with them.

At a basic level, we believe that the Gospel is fundamentally about transformation, not about information. In other words, we follow Christ and we encourage one another to know Him more, to follow His teachings in our actual, everyday lives, and we work to put His Word into action rather than sit around and argue about it from a theological perspective.

> AT A BASIC LEVEL, WE BELIEVE THAT THE GOSPEL IS FUNDAMENTALLY ABOUT TRANSFORMATION, NOT ABOUT INFORMATION.

UNITY OR DIVISION?

I think doctrinal statements divide as equally as they unify. For those who agree, unity. For those who do not, division. But if the church says, "We love Jesus and we're following Him in our daily life." Then all followers of Christ can agree with that and those that don't have no place in the Body, because they are not following Christ.

Even with doctrinal statements, there will always be those who silently disagree but who go along with the program because they don't want to be excluded from the fellowship. You will also eventually discover that although everyone agrees with doctrine X, they don't all see doctrine Y the same way...and now you've got another opportunity to start excluding people and dividing the church.

Our variety of doctrinal backgrounds at our house church hasn't prevented us from "walking together" or serving together or advancing the Gospel together, or serving the poor together, or anything else. If anything, we learn from people who might otherwise be excluded from our fellowship because we welcome anyone who says, "I love Jesus and I am doing my best to follow Him in my daily life by the Grace of God."

> I DON'T WANT TO BE IN A CHURCH WHERE EVERYONE AGREES WITH ME ON EVERYTHING. HOMOGENIZATION ISN'T OUR GOAL. FOLLOWING JESUS, PUTTING HIS TEACHINGS INTO PRACTICE AND ENCOURAGING OTHERS TO FOLLOW HIM IS.

I don't know about the rest of you, but I don't want to be in a church where everyone agrees with me on everything. Homogenization isn't our goal. Following Jesus, putting His teachings into practice and encouraging others to follow Him is.

WHO MAKES DECISIONS IN AN ORGANIC CHURCH?

One of my favorite memories from the early days of our house church was when we asked the children to lead our meeting. We told them in advance so they'd have time to prepare for this special day. We all anticipated this special morning together for several weeks, and then finally the day arrived.

I'll never forget, after our usual breakfast and fellowship time, we all moved into the den for our share time. The kids all sat together and we waited to see what they would do.

Then one of them said, "Ok, does anyone have something to share with the group today?"

At first it threw us off a little, and then someone laughed out loud at the irony of it all as we realized what was happening: We had modelled the open meeting so well that their "leadership" of our meeting looked exactly the same! It wasn't about who was leading. It was only about Jesus and what He was doing in our Body that morning.

As I sit down to write this, I can't help but recall that special morning when the kids taught us an important lesson—and it was the same lesson we had already taught them—Jesus is our only Head.

Some have suggested—even within the House Church Movement—that human leaders (spiritual parents, elders, pastors, etc.) are necessary for a "healthy" organic church to flourish. I don't disagree in theory—but in practice I think it matters a whole lot what those "leaders" do or do not do, if we are going to truly experience the Headship of Christ in our midst.

Leadership is a spiritual gift. It's right there in the New Testament alongside tongues, healing, miracles, teaching, etc. No doubt about that. And, yes, God does provide some who serve as "Pastors" (plural) in the Church.

But what a leader does—or does not—do in the gathering and among the members of the Body makes all the difference in the world.

Some things a leader, pastor, elder *might* do in the gathering are:

- Gently nudge the talkers to wait for the shy ones

- Gently nudge the shy ones to share what God has place on their hearts

- Initiate prayer for someone who is obviously in need or hurting

- Prayerfully remind the church family why we are here

- Point everyone back to Jesus

Here are some things a leader, pastor, elder should *not* do in the gathering:

- Tell people what to do

- Dominate the conversation

- Establish the order of service

- Get in the way of the Holy Spirit

- Attempt to create an environment that caters to their own personal bias

If I had to write a hundred page book about how to lead an open meeting in an Organic Church, it would contain 99 pages of "Things Not To Do" and only about a page of what you should be doing.

Why? Because the more we do, the less room we allow for Jesus to move and work in our midst.

So, who makes decisions in an organic church? The short answer is: Jesus does.

The longer answer would contain a few suggestions about how to facilitate that in the gathering, but essentially you, as a church family, would take the time to pray together and wait on the Lord and see where and how He is leading you to act or move.

It would be faster to simply elect someone to make all those decisions for you. Obviously. But do you want expedience and efficiency, or do you want accuracy and obedience to Christ?

IF YOUR DESIRE IS TO HEAR FROM THE LORD, AND IF YOUR CHURCH FAMILY REALLY WANTS TO EXPERIENCE CHRIST AT THE HEAD OF THE BODY, THEN TOGETHER AS A BODY YOU NEED TO STOP AND LISTEN TO THE HEAD, WHO IS CHRIST. IT'S REALLY THAT SIMPLE.

If your desire is to hear from the Lord, and if your church family really wants to experience Christ at the Head of the Body, then together as a Body you need to stop and listen to the Head, who is Christ. It's really that simple.

There's an African proverb that says: "If you want to go quickly, go alone. If you want to travel far, go together."

I would urge you, as a brother in Christ, not to go quickly, but to go together and to seek the Lord as a Church Family.

Does it work? Yes! It does work. It has worked several times in our own house church family, and it has worked spectacularly for others as well.

For example, one young couple who we know started an organic church recently after visiting with us only a few times. After their group had been together a few months, someone donated a large sum of money to them. Seeing as Organic Churches don't need money to operate, they were unsure of what to do with the money. So, they came together and prayed and asked Jesus what they should do. Here's what happened next:

> "We bowed our heads and a few different people prayed aloud for wisdom and discernment for all of us to come to an agreement on what to do. After a long period of silence, we asked if the Spirit had put any specific direction on anyone's heart. One woman spoke up and said, "I kept thinking of the numbers, 60-30-10" and someone else said, "I sensed the numbers 600, 300, 100," another "60-30-10," and finally, a fourth, "6-3-1, double."

> "The woman who sensed "6-3-1, double" went on to explain that the 6 meant $600 and was to go to one need. The 3 meant $300 and was meant to go to the other need, and the 1 was $100 and needed to be kept back. The she went on and said something like, "The 'double' is because we are meant to give our own money and double what has been given to us because right now this gift hasn't cost us anything and we are meant to give out of our own resources."

> "We returned to group dialogue to check with everyone's spirit to make sure there weren't any "red flags" in anyone's hearts, and, surprisingly, everyone was on the same page. We were then able to discuss how to be people of generosity throughout the week and to plan to "double" what had been given to us by giving back to needs we experienced in our circles of influence.

> "A sense of excitement and peace permeated that living room as we reflected on the fact that the Spirit had spoken, and not only that, but He had chosen to do so through different members of our group while the rest tested His voice. People remarked to one another that they felt a part of something significant and how amazing it was to observe and participate in the body responding to the movement of the Spirit."[1]

The more your organic church practices this sort of thing, the more common and "normal" it will become. But it will only work if everyone in the church family works together to submit to the Holy Spirit, and to one another, to arrive at the answer that the Lord desires for you.

Who makes decisions in an Organic Church? Jesus does! He's the Head. He's the Senior Pastor. The rest of us are all brothers and sisters—and members of His Body—who submit to Christ as Lord, both in our personal lives, and in our corporate times together as a Family.

Once you hand all of this over to an expert or a Senior Pastor, it's the last corporate decision your Church will ever make together.

Do you want to go far? Go together. Just make sure you're all following Jesus.

10 THINGS I'LL DO DIFFERENTLY NEXT TIME WE PLANT A CHURCH

Over the last few years, my wife and I have been helping to facilitate a church which started in our home and has now begun to grow outward into various other expressions recently.

Like most people, what I've learned has mostly come from making mistakes. So, while I'm certain that I'll make more than my own share of new mistakes the next time I plant a church, here are the things I've learned from our first time around. Hopefully this will encourage some of you as you consider planting a house church.

1. DON'T CALL YOURSELF THE PASTOR.

If you're "the pastor" of your house church this means everyone will look to you for everything and it will paralyze the Body life of the Church. Instead, identify yourself as one of the functioning members along with everyone else. Involve others for sharing, teaching, testimonials, etc.

2. DON'T HOST EVERY SINGLE MEETING IN YOUR OWN HOME.

For most of the last few years, my wife and I have hosted a meeting in our home twice a week. That's a lot of meetings. We've only recently started rotating our Sunday gatherings. This allows others to share responsibility and to practice hospitality. The next time we plant a house church (assuming there is a next time), I will encourage others to open their homes as early as possible. As new people join, I will invite them to consider hosting as well. Sharing the hosting responsibility also reinforces the concept that anyone can facilitate the gathering and that they don't need you to be present in order to gather as a Body.

3. INVOLVE THE CHILDREN MORE.

In our group, the children have always shared scriptures alongside the adults and many of the greatest insights have come from elementary-age children. Even so, I wish we had involved them even more in our conversations, in prayer times for one another, in the communion of the Lord's table, etc. I don't think it's really possible to have too much involvement from our kids. House Church provides the perfect opportunity to give our kids a hands-on experience of what it means to "be the Church" every single time we gather.

4. HAVE MORE FUN TOGETHER.

Over the years we've had occasional game nights and a couple of afternoons in the park, but I wish we had scheduled even more times to come together and just be the family of God. No songs, no teaching, no liturgy, just laughing and food and genuine intimacy with one another. Sharing life together is huge and later on as you grow deeper into Christ, those relationships will become even more important and necessary for keeping one another accountable and for loving correction. It's also important to reinforce the idea that we are the Church all the time, not just when we're reading scripture or praying out loud.

5. TALK LESS, QUESTION MORE.

I am plagued by a disease which compels me to answer every single biblical or theological question that anyone asks. I wish I had just shut up whenever a Biblical question came up. Instead of attempting to stun the inquirer with my Biblical expertise, I wish I had turned to the group and said, "I don't know. What do you guys think?"

6. EMPHASIZE THE GOSPEL OF THE KINGDOM MORE.

In my experience, people who really understand the Gospel of the Kingdom are able to grasp all the other concepts of the Kingdom more easily. I wish I had spent more time emphasizing that in our fellowship, and I know I will major on this more and more in the future.

7. MAJOR ON PRACTICING OUR FAITH AND LESS ON THEORIZING.

Being the Church is so much more necessary than attending one. Because this is one of the core values of New Testament Church life, I would encourage everyone to live out their faith in more practical ways in the future—and make more room for sharing testimony and for continually challenging everyone to do so daily.

8. PRAY MORE.

Jesus said that His house would be a house of prayer. If we are His Body, and the Temple of the Holy Spirit, then we should be on our faces before God more and more. "An open meeting requires more time in prayer together, not less." That's why I would encourage every home church to gather for prayer as often as possible. Jesus is our Head, without Him we can do nothing. That's why we need to be on our knees, seeking His leadership and listening for His voice.

9. CONFESS MY OWN WEAKNESSES MORE.

For too long I've kept my own personal struggles to myself instead of opening up to the rest of the Body whenever I felt hurt, or depressed, or discouraged. My wife knew when I was having a hard time with things, but the church was mostly oblivious. In the future, I will openly confess my struggles and allow the Body to comfort me and to heal me and to strengthen me.

10. SHARE THE DUTIES OF SACRAMENT WITH THE PRIESTHOOD OF ALL BELIEVERS.

In our next house church, I will not perform the baptisms. Instead, I will encourage the Body to operate as equals and to baptize one another and to take turns leading all of us in Lord's Supper together. Again, if I am the one doing these things, I am behaving like the "pastor" or the spiritual superior and that's the last thing I want to communicate. Instead, I'd want to emphasize the truth that any follower of Jesus is already ordained by the Holy Spirit of God to preach the Gospel, baptize new believers and administer the Lord's Supper to the saints—among other things. The less I am up front, the more the Body can be empowered to step into their priesthood and utilize their gifts in love.

Of course, all of this presumes that I will ever help to plant another church in the future. I'm not sure if I ever will, but if not, perhaps some of this advice can encourage those of you who are feeling called to step out in faith and follow God's calling on your life to do so.

The single best piece of advice I can offer is this: Stop trying to grow the Church on your own. That's not your job. Jesus said that He would grow His Church, and over the last five years I've learned that this is exactly what He will do...if we can get out of His way.

CHAPTER 8

HOW TO HAVE A MEETING WITH JESUS (NOT JUST ABOUT HIM)

IS IT REALLY ALL ABOUT JESUS?

For me, the essence of an Organic Church is centered around Jesus. Everything we do should be designed to help us hear Him, experience Him, worship Him, love Him, serve Him, and draw nearer to Him. Anything that prevents that from happening should be eliminated from our lives, and from our time together as a Body.

If I could re-name the movement, I'd call it "Jesus Ekklesia" because, for me, that's closer to what it's all about: It's for Jesus, by Jesus and of Jesus. With Jesus at the Center, Jesus at the top, and Jesus surrounding us, the Ekklesia is a Jesus-centric organism that won't operate properly apart from Jesus.

In fact, the Church itself is nothing apart from Christ. The Apostle Paul calls it a Profound Mystery. Christ and the Church are One—like a living person who has a head and a body and organs that all work together to sustain life. We are in Christ and He is in us, and we are the Temple of the Holy Spirit where Christ lives, and He is the One in whom we live and move and have our being. So, we are in Christ and He is in us, and we are in the Father.

Apart from Jesus we can do nothing. Yet, if we remain in Him and He remains in us then we will bear much fruit.

Is it possible to have a meeting without Jesus? Unfortunately, yes. It's also possible to have a wonderful meeting "about Jesus" where people get together to sing about Him, talk about Him and study Him—much in the same way a group of people might study any other topic of discussion.

BUT RATHER THAN HAVE A MEETING "ABOUT JESUS", OR A MEETING "WITHOUT JESUS", OUR AIM AND PURPOSE SHOULD ALWAYS BE TO HAVE A MEETING "WITH JESUS."

But rather than have a meeting "about Jesus", or a meeting "without Jesus", our aim and purpose should always be to have a meeting "*with* Jesus." He is the One we want to hear from. He is the One we want to touch, and to see and to experience.

Keep in mind, it's possible to know stuff about someone without actually knowing the person. For example, I could know all sorts of trivia about Kobe Bryant, but if he walked in the room he wouldn't say, "Hello Keith!" because I don't actually know Kobe Bryant. I only know stuff about him.

The same is true for Christianity. We can know lots of stuff about Jesus, but that does not mean that we actually know Jesus in an intimate, relational way.

But how do we do that? How do we take hold of Christ—or allow Him to take hold of us?

I mean, if I'm not connecting with the actual Jesus in my private life, then I'm certainly not going to be able to connect with Him in a room full of people.

And, of course, if I'm in a room full of people who are also not in connection with the actual person of Jesus, then even if I am connected to Him, their limited connection to Him will probably make it impossible for all of us to encounter Him together.

How do we connect with Jesus as individuals? How do individual Christians encounter Jesus when they come together as a Church?

Those are the big questions, aren't they? I'll do my best to answer both of those questions.

INDIVIDUAL CONNECTIONS TO CHRIST

One of the most important things Jesus ever said about the Christian life was this: "Abide in me and I will abide in you. Apart from me you can do nothing."

So, our individual connection to Jesus begins with living in Him. Not just placing our faith in Him, or trusting in Him for salvation, but actually living and breathing in Christ daily.

Or, to put it another way, the Christian life is about allowing Jesus to come and live and breathe in you every moment of every day.

Imagine an empty water bottle with the lid screwed on tight. It's full of air. Now throw it into the ocean. It's surrounded by water, but on the inside it's still empty and dry. That's sort of like what it can be like for Christians who find themselves surrounded by Christian "things" and ideas, or even in a gathering of other Christians, but on the inside they are still empty and dry.

Even if you were to submerge that bottle deep into the center of the ocean, it would be wet on the outside, but dry on the inside. What needs to happen is for the bottle to be opened up so that the ocean can come flooding inside.

Jesus is the Ocean. We are the bottle. We can get close to Him and still not let Him inside. Total surrender is required for transformation to begin.

And I say, "to begin" because this is a process not a onetime event.

We allow the process to begin when we surrender our lives to Jesus, die to everything that is our self, and open our hearts up to receive His life, and His heart, and His presence.

We do not ask Jesus into our life, which is empty and dry and weak, but instead we respond to Jesus as He invites us into His life which is pure and eternal and abundant.

The Christian life is cultivated and nurtured and celebrated daily. We spend time with Jesus. We talk to Him the way we talk to our closest friend. We ask Him daily for help as we put His words into practice. We lean on Him for wisdom. We turn to Him for comfort. We look to Him for everything.

Keep in mind that practicing the presence of God like this will likely impact your behavior. It will facilitate the transformational power of the Holy Spirit as you open yourself up more and more to His command and control.

Any Christian who is consumed by this sort of attitude and activity can't help but experience more of Jesus in their daily life. Now just imagine what would happen if a dozen or so other Christians who were also practicing this sort of faith were to get together for a meeting with Jesus as their functional head?

That's what Organic Church is all about.

CORPORATE CONNECTIONS TO CHRIST

When followers of Jesus are accustomed to encountering Jesus like this seven days a week, it's nothing out of the ordinary to put something very similar into practice when they gather with others who are familiar with the concept.

The New Testament describes for us in some detail what a gathering of the Body of Christ should look like. In 1 Corinthians

12 through 14, Paul talks about the Church using the metaphor of a body where the head (which is Christ) controls every member of his body (the members of the church) as they operate together in ways that are various but necessary to the overall health of the entire organism.

This means that a church is really only "the Body of Christ" if it is submitted fully to the Head. If any church is not operating so that Christ alone is the functional leader—and everyone in the church is operating in their gifting as directed by the Holy Spirit—then that church is not actually behaving like a Body. It might be acting like a corporate entity, a 501(c)3, a business, or a bible study, but it's not a Body.

When a group of practicing Christian disciples gather together under Christ in order to see Him and hear Him and encounter Him, the chances of doing so increase exponentially.

> IT MIGHT BE ACTING LIKE A CORPORATE ENTITY, A 501(C)3, A BUSINESS, OR A BIBLE STUDY, BUT IT'S NOT A BODY.

Obviously, if Christians are not practicing a daily surrender to Christ in their personal lives, and if they are not gathering with other Christians who are encountering Jesus in this way, and if when they gather together they don't all work together to experience Jesus in their midst as their functional head...then there's a very, very good chance that they won't.

Having said that, let me admit something here: It doesn't always come together for us either.

Sometimes we realize that we've not been walking as close to Jesus as we should. Sometimes we get together and we discover that most of us have neglected to seek His face during the week—hey, it happens. We're all human. We get distracted. We get busy. We fall back into old habits and formulas.

At other times we find that one person in the group isn't as focused on seeking Him as the rest of us are. In those cases we have grace. We wait for them. We ask how they're doing. We minister to them in love.

We don't compare ourselves to them as if we are more holy than they are. Mostly because we remember that we ourselves are prone to the same failures and weaknesses.

Still at other times we can all be in the right place at the right time and with the same intention and yet we don't experience the power and presence of Jesus the way we hoped we might.

Again, that's ok. Our faith isn't in an experience. Our faith and our hope is in a person. We trust Him and we wait for Him. If He decides to move among us, then we rejoice and we receive. If He decides to remain silent, then we continue to wait on Him.

I think sometimes Jesus changes things up simply to keep us from relying on formulas. People love formulas. But when we have a formula we don't need God.

Church isn't about a formula, it is (once again) about a person. Jesus is a person and so we learn to accommodate Him and to defer to Him and to relate to Him as a person, not as a formula.

A PRACTICAL EXAMPLE

Here's an example of how our little group experienced the Headship of Christ—and it was really wonderful.

After our singing time, one of our sisters shared about a message she had seen on someone's t-shirt at the grocery store the previous week. It said "Live what you love" and that little phrase stuck with her all week. She began to meditate on how we should live our lives for Jesus and follow Him because He is the One we love.

After that, another sister shared two verses from the New Testament about love and talked about how the Lord had revealed more of His love to her that week.

Then I jumped in because that morning I had been reading through 1 John which is all about love and I read a few specific verses from that book and shared my perspective on how important it is that we learn to love one another.

Then one of our brothers shared what God had been showing him last week as he read through the book of Hosea. After that another brother shared what God had been showing him as he was reading a book about the prophet Hosea, which dove-tailed beautifully into what everyone else was already sharing.

We ended by praying for one of our other sisters who shared a little from her heart about needing to be reminded of the love of God for her—which is what we had all been talking about all morning long anyway!

As we laid hands on her, and read scriptures over her, and even sang songs over her of God's amazing and astounding love for her, everyone was edified and blessed and touched by the Lord's tender presence with us.

That was an incredible morning with the saints! And I wish I could tell you that it happens like that every single week, but it doesn't.

The good news is that it's starting to happen more and more often as we all begin to catch a vision for what the Lord intends for us as individuals and as a corporate Body of believers.

ORGANIC CHURCH FLOW CHART

Here's a very simple flow chart for how to have a meeting with Jesus, and not just a meeting about Jesus.

You don't need to follow this exactly, but it's a good starting point to help guide your meetings with Jesus.

FELLOWSHIP

This is a very natural, and important, part of house church. As people arrive, share some tea, or coffee and feel free to let everyone talk without feeling the need to guide or control the conversations. Just let everyone find their rhythm.

This can be 15 to 20 minutes as you wait for people to show up.

JESUS TIME

This begins with an extended period of silence. You might want to explain to everyone what you're doing and why—especially if there are new people joining you. Let them know that it's not only ok for their to be long periods of silence, this is actually what you are wanting to experience together.

The idea at first is for everyone to simply stop and recognize the presence of Jesus in your midst. He has always been there, but now what you're doing all together is to actually acknowledge his presence and to celebrate it.

When and if anyone speaks, it should be to Jesus, not to one another. So, for example, someone might say, "Jesus, thank you for loving us. Thank you for your presence here with all of us today. We're so grateful that you are faithful, and we need you."

Someone may feel like reading a verse of scripture, and hopefully it's something that points us to Jesus, or reminds us of his love, or his goodness, or his peace.

A few verses that we have enjoyed reading out loud during this time are Colossians 1:15-22; Romans 8:31-39; Revelation 5 (the whole chapter); Hebrews 1:1-13; Ephesians 3: 14-21.

These are only a few to get you started, but eventually your group will begin to find their own favorite verses to read as everyone is basking in the presence of Jesus together.

Remember: Long periods of silence are acceptable and even encouraged. Give everyone time to listen to the Holy Spirit, and to respond to Jesus in their own way.

REMEMBER: LONG PERIODS OF SILENCE ARE ACCEPTABLE AND EVEN ENCOURAGED. GIVE EVERYONE TIME TO LISTEN TO THE HOLY SPIRIT, AND TO RESPOND TO JESUS IN THEIR OWN WAY.

Please, also try beforehand to remind everyone not to overshare. The idea is to give everyone an opportunity to participate. So, if you're talking that means you're taking someone else's time. Keep it short, simple and sweet.

WORSHIP SONGS

Eventually, someone might want to sing a song of worship or thanksgiving to Jesus. This can be done without music, or maybe if someone plays guitar and can play the song in question it can be handled that way.

Sometimes it's ok to have someone play a song on their iPhone off of YouTube if that's your only option. Just be careful to mute the commercials first.

OPEN SHARE TIME

A lot of house church groups are already familiar with this. It's where everyone is free to share whatever the Lord has given them—as long as it is something that really encourages and lifts up the Body of Christ. This should not be a gripe session, nor should it be a long Bible study on a particular passage.

The idea is to share something that God has been teaching you during the week, or a thought, idea, or lesson that the Lord has shown you—perhaps even as you were all waiting on the Lord during your silent time together. But, the idea is that we share things that are practical, genuine, and intended to help everyone in their own daily walk with Christ.

Remember, whatever you share, keep it short. Everyone needs an opportunity to respond, or to share something of their own. This is part of what it means to honor one another over yourself.

Often, I use the potluck model as an illustration. If I invited people over to my house for a potluck dinner and everyone brought crackers, an orange, and some pop-tarts, we'd have a pretty awful potluck dinner, right?

But, if everyone decided to really put some thought into what they wanted to bring, and found a recipe, and went shopping for the ingredients during the week, and prepared the dish just in time to bring it over, still warm from the oven, we'd all have an amazing feast.

This is exactly like the open share time. If we take no time to think about it, or to prepare to bring something special that could really bless our brothers and sisters, then everyone will suffer. But, if we really do take the time to pray, prepare, and bring something that we can share in love because we want to be a blessing to our brothers and sisters in Christ, then that open share time will be rich and rewarding for everyone.

IN THE OLD WAY OF DOING CHURCH, WE USED TO DRIVE TO THE SERVICE WONDERING IF WE'D GET BLESSED, AND WE'D DRIVE HOME EITHER COMPLAINING THAT WE WEREN'T, OR THANKFUL THAT WE WERE.

In the old way of doing church, we used to drive to the service wondering if we'd get blessed, and we'd drive home either complaining that we weren't, or thankful that we were. But in a house church it's the opposite. We drive to house church hoping that we can BE a blessing to everyone else. And if everyone who comes to house church arrives fully prepared to be a blessing, then guess what? Everyone leaves with a blessing! Even if that blessing was the joy that comes from knowing that you got to bless someone else.

MINISTRY TIME

This is where we take time to lay hands on one another and pray for healing, or encouragement, for blessing, or whatever is needed. We may speak words of blessing over one another, or wash one another's feet—either figuratively or literally. We may go around the room and tell one another what we love most about them. We may read verses of scripture over each other, or tell someone how much we can see Jesus in them.

Whatever it happens to look like, the entire point is to lift one another up in Christ.

BREAKING BREAD

You can eat at the beginning of your meeting, or at the end. Our group has done both, but we preferred eating at the end. This also allowed us more time to fellowship and continue to share our lives with one another.

If you like, you can share communion together, either before the end of your share time, or during the actual meal time. It's up to you.

Once again, your meeting doesn't have to look exactly like this. In fact, it probably shouldn't. Otherwise it wouldn't be organic, would it?

THE HOUSE OF ELEVEN WINDOWS

A little over 11 years ago, my wife Wendy and I responded to a calling that, at first, sounded impossible: To start a church that gives everything away.

That idea came after we had accepted the Lord's calling to leave the church we had helped to start only 3 years previously, to plant a brand-new church here in Orange County, California.

The first idea was exhilarating. The second idea seemed impossible.

"How will I support my family?" I wondered.

The idea of a church that gives everything away—keeping nothing for rent, or donuts, or sound systems or staff, or pastoral salaries—was exactly what the first century Christians did with their money. But to do this in Orange County, in 2006, seemed a little...insane.

But, we were convinced that this was indeed what God was calling us to do. So, we took that huge step and did exactly that.

Early on, even before we started our house church, a dear old woman named Ethel gave us a word from the Lord which greatly encouraged us. Even though she had no idea that we were leaving to start a house church, the Lord had shown her a picture of a house with eleven windows one morning as she was praying for us. When she asked the Lord about it, He said, "I'm going to bless this family with eleven windows of opportunity."

That word propelled us forward with even more joy and expectation for what God might be calling us to do. So, we took that huge step and quit our jobs at the church in Tustin to start a church that gives everything away to the poor.

We called it "The Mission" and our conviction was that we were all missionaries with a unique and personal mission to glorify Jesus in our corner of the world.

It took an entire year for me to find a full-time job to support our family. But it was worth it! We loved taking every single penny placed in the offering basket at the back of the room and using it to buy groceries for our new friends who lived in the motel in Santa Ana, just down the road.

We loved giving away money to single moms who were in need, or struggling families who needed help with rent, or homeless old men who needed a place to sleep at night.

We also loved the people that found us and decided to call our little fellowship "home."

They, of course, made it home for us, too. Their insights, their honesty, their compassion, their laughter, and their unique gifts were what made gathering together so sweet for everyone.

We also loved that every single person—young or old, male or female—was free to share from their own experience of Christ. Discipleship for us was our every moment of life, every breath we took, every day we lived our lives and went to work and drove the freeways and interacted with people around us.

From the very beginning every assumption we had about what church was supposed to be, or what leadership looked like, or what following Jesus was all about, was totally challenged and transformed from the inside out.

For the record: I was not the senior pastor of this church. Jesus was. I did not set the agenda. Jesus did. I did not lead the gatherings or take control of the meeting. Jesus did. I did not do all of the talking, or teaching, or speaking. The Body of Christ did, as directed by the Holy Spirit within them.

In fact, there were many gatherings when I was not even present, and often if I was present I would intentionally leave the room (especially in the beginning) and would not return until I heard everyone else sharing freely what the Lord had given them to share.

We took very seriously the idea that we could have a meeting *with* Jesus and not just have a meeting *about* Jesus. We also believed that being the Church was more important than going to Church.

We especially loved inviting people to join our fellowship. That meant the poor, the homeless, the outcasts, the misfits, gay or straight people—even at times Muslims and unbelievers of all kinds—were all welcome in our homes and at our table.

We also loved bringing free groceries to our friends who lived at the motel in Santa Ana one Saturday every month, and sharing breakfast and the Gospel of Christ with them one Sunday each month.

We loved praying with our friends who lived in Tent City, just about a mile down the road from my house, in the shadow of Angel Stadium, and learning to receive love as much as we shared love with those dear people who had nothing but love to give.

One morning I was praying and reflecting on all that God had done to that point through our House Church, and I was reminded of that word about the House of Eleven Windows. God whispered to me: "How many windows are in your house?"

As I mentally began to count them I realized: Our house had eleven windows! What's more: Our friend Ethel had never seen or been inside this house.

So, God's word for us was specifically about this house—the one we were living in and hosting house church in. But that wasn't all.

We also started to get to know our neighbors. Right away we started hosting Kids Club in our home and invited all the kids from the neighborhood to join us during the summer. We hosted Pancake Breakfasts in our driveway on July 4th and invited all of our neighbors to come and get to know one another—which was such a blast that everyone insisted we do it every year—so we did.

We also started inviting our next door neighbors (who were Hindu and Catholic) over for dinner, and then for our Passover Seder celebration, and then just for fun.

Our two sons also started taking out the garbage cans every week for our elderly neighbors on the other side of us, causing another young man on our street to volunteer to take them in every morning after they were emptied.

We discovered the natural presence of Christ in every conversation, and in every smile. Sometimes we prayed for our neighbors when they were going through a divorce. Other times we held their hands as the ambulance pulled away from their house with their loved ones inside.

One night we had an angel at our door—literally "Angelica"— who had run away from a girl's home and had nowhere to go.

I could tell you so many more stories. But the main thing I have to tell you is this: those "eleven windows of opportunity" were about more than we first believed.

Our first clue came when things at the Motel Church began winding down. Then God closed the door. Next, the Tent City was removed by court order. Then, one by one, people in our house church began coming to us with tears of joy, and sadness, to let us know that God was calling them to leave and start another expression of His Kingdom somewhere else.

We prayed with them. We encouraged them. We let them know how proud we were. And then we sent them out.

That's when I realized that all of this started eleven years ago, and that God's word for us about "eleven windows" was about how long we had to serve.

Last week, (as I write this), I took a job in Idaho. We leave at the end of this month.

My final gathering with our house church will be this Sunday. After eleven years, our windows of opportunity here in this house, and in California, are coming to a close.

A few days ago, as I was driving home after dropping off another load of books and clothes to the Salvation Army, I felt the Lord whisper to me: "Mission accomplished" and I just lost it.

Tears rolled down my face as an endless flood of faces, and people, and memories began to flash through my mind. I saw all the people we touched, all the lives we blessed, all the experiences that changed us, and all the wonder of Christ expressed through each person who called this gathering their home. It was almost too much to bear; almost too wonderful to take in at once.

I felt my Abba Father wrap his arms around my shoulders and weep with me for the joy, and the breathtaking beauty of it all.

"Mission accomplished," he said.

And I knew it was true.

So, our mission in Orange County, is now over. This book you're holding is a byproduct of that experience. I hope it has blessed you, and I sincerely hope that you are inspired by what is shared here enough to put some of these ideas into practice in your own home, and in your own community.

This idea of ekklesia is beautiful. It's transformational. It's God great design to change the world from the inside out into people who look and act and love like Jesus.

I long for the day when the Bride of Christ fully awakens to this idea of ekklesia as God intended.

I hope I live to see it spread to every tribe and tongue and nation.

I hope you do, too.

Blessings,

– Keith

ENDNOTES

INTRODUCTION

1. Tozer, A.W., *The Knowledge of the Holy*, 1978, p. 79

CHAPTER 1

1. From "Interview with Dr. G.K. Beale, Part 1" on June 6, 2009 at www. KeithGiles.com

2. From the article, "A Better Covenant, Priesthood and Hope" by A.W. Tozer

3. Ketcherside, W. Carl, *The Royal Priesthood*, Chapter 11

4. Snyder, Howard, *Christ's Body: The Community of the King*, 1977, pp.94-95

5. Bausch, William, *Traditions, Tensions, Transitions in Ministry*, Twenty-Third Publications

6. Haag, Herbert, *Upstairs, Downstairs: Did Jesus Want a Two-Class Church?*, 1997, p.109

7. McNeal, Reggie, *The Present Future*, 2009, p.4

8. From *Provocations: Spiritual Writings of Kierkegaard*, edited by Charles Moore

9. An excerpt from Tertullian's "Apology," taken from *Roman Civilization Sourcebook II: The Empire*, p.588

10. From the article, "Listening to Your Life", Harper, 1992, p.331

11. From the book, *Tozer on Christian Leadership*, Christian Publications, 2001

12. Simson, Wolfgang, *Houses That Change The World*, p. 208

13. Scott, Ernest F., *The Nature of the Early Church*, Charles Scribner's Sons, 1941, pp.75-87

14. Ketcherside, W. Carl, *The Royal Priesthood*, Chapter 11

CHAPTER 2

1. Quote by Richard Halverson, former Chaplain of the United States Senate

2. Yoder, John H., *The Fullness of Christ*

CHAPTER 3

1. From the blog article published June 23, 2009 at www.alanknox.net/2009/06/the-birth-and-growth-of-a-church/

CHAPTER 6

1. For additional insights, read my e-book *How to Start A Ministry to the Poor in Your Community* on Amazon.com

CHAPTER 7

1. From the blog post "Sixty, Thirty, Ten, Double" by Christa MicKirland

For more information about Keith Giles
or to contact him for speaking engagements,
please visit *www.KeithGiles.com*

Many voices. One message.

Quoir is a boutique publisher
with a singular message: *Christ is all.*
Venture beyond your boundaries to discover Christ
in ways you never thought possible.

For more information, please visit
www.quoir.com

HERETIC HAPPY HOUR

Burning questions, not people.

Heretic Happy Hour is an unapologetically irreverent, crass, and sometimes profound conversation about the Christian faith. Hosts, Matthew Distefano, Jamal Jivanjee, and Keith Giles pull no punches and leave no stones unturned. For some serious sacred cow-tipping, there's nothing better than spending an hour of your time with us.

www.heretichappyhour.com